engage

Welcome to the smiley happy fi.... ....
As usual, it's packed with top quality Bible teaching
and some brain-scramblingly challenging articles.
Check out what's in store for you in this issue...

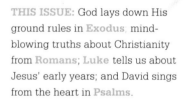

✱ DAILY READINGS Each day's
page throws you into the Bible, to
get you handling, questioning and
exploring God's message to you —
encouraging you to act on it and talk
to God more in prayer.

THIS ISSUE: God lays down His
ground rules in Exodus; mind-
blowing truths about Christianity
from Romans; Luke tells us about
Jesus' early years; and David sings
from the heart in Psalms.

✱ TAKE IT FURTHER If you're
hungry for more at the end of an
engage page, turn to the Take it
further section to dig deeper.

✱ STUFF Articles on stuff relevant
to the lives of young Christians. This
issue: what does the Bible have to say
about alcohol and drugs?

✱ TRICKY tackles those mind-
bendingly tricky questions that
confuse us all, as well as questions
that our friends bombard us with.
This time: What happens to people
who have never heard the gospel?

✱ ESSENTIAL Articles on the
basics we really need to know about
God, the Bible and Christianity. This
issue: The Bible – can we trust it?

✱ REAL LIVES True stories,
revealing God at work in people's
lives. This time — A teenage
Christian with a serious illness.

✱ TOOLBOX is full of tools to
help you wrestle with the Bible
and understand it for yourself.
This issue we look at the Bible
and say 'So what?'

All of us who work on engage are
passionate to see God's word at
work in people's lives. Do you
want God's word to have an
impact on your life? Then open
your Bible, and start on the first
engage study right now...

HOW TO USE engage

1 Set a time you can read the Bible every day

2 Find a place where you can be quiet and think

3 Grab your Bible, pen and a notebook

4 Ask God to help you understand what you read

5 Read the day's verses with engage, taking time to think about it

6 Pray about what you've read

BIBLE STUFF We use the NIV Bible version, so you might find it's the best one to use with engage. If the notes say **'Read Exodus 16 v 1–12'**, look up Exodus in the contents page at the front of your Bible. It'll tell you which page Exodus starts on. Find chapter 16 of Exodus, and then verse 1 of chapter 16 (the verse numbers are the tiny ones). Then start reading. Simple.

In this issue...

ENGAGE BRAINIACS

Scintillating scribes: Martin Cole   Cassie Martin   Fiona Simmons   Sarah Smart   Tim Thornborough   Helen Thorne

Bionic editor: Martin Cole

Hi-tech design: Steve Devane

Precise proof-reading: Anne Woodcock

Exodus

The big clean-up

You've finally left home. And you're about to start sharing a house with your best friends in the whole world, Barry and Flo — it's going to be great! But there are a few issues you need to sort out first...

HOUSE RULES

To begin with, the house is a total mess; in fact it's a disaster zone. There's no way you could live there until some serious cleaning takes place. Barry, bless him, hasn't ever grasped the concept of washing up and wouldn't know which end of a vacuum cleaner was which.

And there's also the matter of setting some ground rules, like taking it in turns to buy the milk, how to pay shared bills and who cleans the bathroom. But once things are clean and you've sorted out the house rules, it's going to be awesome living with these guys!

You're probably thinking: *'What does this have to do with the second half of Exodus??!'*

THE STORY SO FAR

God's people have been rescued from slavery in Egypt with some astounding displays of God's power. But what have they been rescued for? Well, God intends to fulfil all His promises to Abraham — promises of a land to live in, a great nation of people and blessing. As God starts to do that, one big part of the blessing is that He will live among them.

However, just like Barry and Flo, the Israelites have got some serious cleaning up to do before a pure and holy God can live with such a sinful bunch of people. And God is going to give them some ground rules about how it will all work.

So read on to see how this incredible 'house share' began.

1 | Short-term memory

It's six weeks after Operation Exodus when God rescued His people from slavery in Egypt. Under Moses' leadership, the Israelites are headed for the Promised Land. But it's not going to be a straightforward journey...

◉ Read Exodus 16 v 1–12

ENGAGE YOUR BRAIN

▷ *Why are the Israelites grumbling? (v3)*

▷ *What are their rose-tinted memories of Egypt? (v3)*

Hang on a minute! Is this the same place we're talking about? The one where you were in terrible slavery, where the country's ruler wanted to kill all your baby boys? Get real!

GET ON WITH IT

Be honest with yourself. Do you ever catch yourself thinking: *'Life would be so much easier if I wasn't a Christian. I could get drunk, date that guy/girl or sleep with them, spend my money on whatever I wanted, sleep in on Sunday mornings...'*? Missing your old sinful ways? Don't fool yourself — life without God is slavery and it ends in death. Don't slip into that way of thinking; it's very dangerous.

▷ *Who are the people grumbling about? (v2)*

▷ *Are you sure? (v8)*

▷ *What might you expect God's reaction to be?*

▷ *What is His reaction? (v4, v12)*

How amazing is that? Instead of blasting them into oblivion, God kindly provides them with bread and meat.

▷ *What does He want the Israelites to remember? (v12)*

PRAY ABOUT IT

Do you know that the LORD is your God? Really know it? Think about who He is — kind and gracious, compassionate and slow to anger — and then thank Him that trusting in Jesus means He is your God too.

THE BOTTOM LINE

Don't wish for life without God.

→ TAKE IT FURTHER

Escape from slavery on page 108.

2 Birds and bread

All that grumbling must have given the Israelites an appetite. Just as He promised, God provides quail — a posh sort of pheasant — and supernatural bread from heaven. Dig in!

👁 Read Exodus 16 v 13–36

ENGAGE YOUR BRAIN

▶ What food does God provide in the evening? And the morning?

▶ What instructions does Moses give about collecting the manna? v16:

v19:

v22–23:

▶ What happens when the people don't follow those instructions?

▶ What is God trying to teach His people about Himself? (v28-29)

▶ How long will it take them to learn that? (v32, v35)

We might think that the Israelites were incredibly slow on the uptake — of course God knew what they needed and of course He would provide for them as He'd promised.

Why on earth didn't they trust Him?

PRAY ABOUT IT

Take a minute to ask yourself the same question and answer it honestly. Why don't you always trust God? Talk to God about your answer and ask Him to help you trust Him more.

GET ON WITH IT

Is there something in your life that you know God wants you to do or stop doing? Will you take Him seriously and obey Him?

THE BOTTOM LINE

Trusting God means doing what He says.

➡ TAKE IT FURTHER

Get your daily bread on page 108.

3 | Rock on!

Imagine the situation. You've seen God do amazing miracles to rescue you. He's guiding you personally by day and night and is providing wonderful supernatural food for you every day. Then you get a bit thirsty...

👁 Read Exodus 17 v 1–7

ENGAGE YOUR BRAIN

▷ *Read verse one again. What should the people have done?*

▷ *What did they do? (v2)*

▷ *Again, who are they really having a go at? (v2, v7)*

▷ *Why is v7 so shocking?*

▷ *What is Moses' response to the situation? (v4)*

Pray or pout? Turn to God or turn against him? Every time they encounter a difficulty the Israelites just moan. That's not to say there wasn't a real need, but their response was all wrong. Moses gets it right — he takes his problems straight to God. And notice he's not doing so in a calm and super spiritual manner — he's complaining too. BUT Moses addresses his complaints to the One who can do something about them!

PRAY ABOUT IT

Are you tempted to complain rather than pray when things are tough? Spend some time now asking for God's help with the difficulties you face. Say sorry for the times you moan about life.

▷ *Sum up in a word God's response to these grumblers in v6–7:*

Incredibly God once again meets the needs of this bunch of moaners and in a very strange way — did you notice v6? In some way God is present there in front of Moses and provides the water they need to live — more on this in the *Take It Further* section.

THE BOTTOM LINE

If you want to complain — take your complaints to the top, to God.

→ TAKE IT FURTHER

More on talking honestly with God on page 108.

4 | Hands up!

The Israelites faced lack of food and water and God provided for their needs every step of the way. But in these next few verses they face a new threat.

👁 Read Exodus 17 v 8–16

ENGAGE YOUR BRAIN

▶ *What danger does Israel face in v8?*

The Amalekites were a nasty bunch — one of their preferred strategies was to lurk behind straggling travellers and attack the old and weak (Deuteronomy 25 v 17–18).

▶ *What is the outcome of the battle and how does it come about?*

It's not quite clear what Moses is doing with his hands in the air — he could be praying or he could be signalling the troops to advance rather than retreat. Moses mentions that it's the staff of God he's holding, which makes it very clear that he is relying totally on God.

▶ *What is God's promise to Moses about Israel's enemy? (v14)*

▶ *Who does Moses give all the credit to? (v16)*

Moses put his trust firmly in God to rescue His people and defend them. He calls the Lord his banner — maybe our equivalent would be a football scarf or a t-shirt that shows where your loyalties lie.

PRAY ABOUT IT

Ask God for His help to stand firm, trusting in Him for everything today. Thank Him for other Christians you know who help you to stand firm.

THE BOTTOM LINE

Is the Lord your banner?

➡ TAKE IT FURTHER

Wave your banner on page 108.

5 | In-laws and outlaws

No major crisis for the Israelites today — phew! At last, they can concentrate on normal stuff like family reunions and daily business.

Read Exodus 18 v 1–12

ENGAGE YOUR BRAIN

▷ Who turns up to see Moses?

▷ What does Moses' choice of names for his kids tell us about:
a) God?
b) Moses' attitude to God?

We don't know much about Jethro's religion, despite him being called the 'priest' of Midian. But he certainly ends up worshipping the Lord here.

▷ What is so great about the topic of Moses' and Jethro's conversation (v7-12)?

SHARE IT

Have you ever tried telling others about the amazing things God has done for you both now and in the past? Not just your Christian mates, but all your friends?

Read verses 13–27

▷ Why is Moses' father-in-law so dumbfounded? (v14)

▷ What is Moses doing (v13, v15–16) and why is it so full-on?

▷ What is Jethro's advice? Do you think it sounds sensible?

Sometimes we're not keen to take advice from people — how do we know they're right? What if they're not even Christians? Notice the key thing about Jethro's advice: not only is it sensible (Moses is headed for exhaustion), but it's God-centred (see v19-21, v23).

PRAY ABOUT IT

Thank God for people who look out for you and give you good advice.

THE BOTTOM LINE

God should get the glory in the big things and the small things.

➡ TAKE IT FURTHER

For a reminder, turn to page 109.

6 | Get ready

Chances are you've heard of what happened on Mount Sinai (if not, read on), so we know from v2 that something pretty special is coming up, but the build-up alone in this chapter is mind-blowing. Check it out...

👁 Read Exodus 19 v 1–6

ENGAGE YOUR BRAIN

▶ What does God remind the Israelites about Himself in v4–6?

▶ What does He promise them in those verses?

▶ How would you describe this relationship?

This is amazing stuff — God is offering these people an incredible privilege, not because they are anything special but because He loves them. That's what the Bible calls **grace** — God's undeserved kindness.

👁 Read verses 7–25

▶ How do the people respond? (v8)

▶ What strikes you most about the preparations which need to be made for God to communicate with human beings? (v10–24)

God is incomprehensibly holy. He is so perfect that without limits and safety barriers, we would be destroyed by His burning perfection. All of the descriptions used — thunder, lightning, darkness, earthquakes, fire and loud noise serve to highlight how immensely powerful and terrifying God is.

PRAY ABOUT IT

Do you realise that God is like this? Spend some time reflecting on these verses again as you talk to Him.

PRAY ABOUT IT SOME MORE

And yet God wants to communicate with us; this terrifying God is the same one who calls His people His *'treasured possession'*. Thank Him.

THE BOTTOM LINE

God is holy. He's a God of grace. Praise Him.

➡ TAKE IT FURTHER

There's more on page 109.

7 | Starter for ten

We might think we know the Ten Commandments: 'Thou shalt not blah, blah, blah'. But look again at the way they begin. Everything God expects of His people is based on understanding His character and His relationship with them.

👁 Read Exodus 20 v 1–6

ENGAGE YOUR BRAIN

▶ List the three things God says about Himself in verses 2, 5 & 6.

1.
2.
3.

When you see *'the LORD'* in the Bible, it means the special name of God which He revealed to Moses – *'I Am'*. It means the only God, the eternal God, who is the same yesterday, today and forever.

▶ What words would you use to define the relationship God has with His people? (v5–6)

▶ What does God forbid them to do?

GET ON WITH IT

Do you have any gods or idols that you worship in the place of the true and living God? Is there something that gets in the way of loving God wholeheartedly? Popularity? Sport? Entertainment? Friends? A boyfriend or girlfriend? Or even your own selfishness? Pray for God's help and get rid of them – ruthlessly.

▶ Why do you think God is so serious about the consequence of not putting Him first? (v5)

The statements that God makes about Himself in v5 and v6 seem very different. But God is good and holy (not overlooking sin) as well as being compassionate and faithful (showing love to a thousand generations).

PRAY ABOUT IT

Ask for God's help to love Him and keep His commandments — not just these ten but everything that Jesus summed up in these words: *'Love the Lord your God with all your heart, soul, mind and strength'* and *'Love your neighbour as yourself'*.

→ TAKE IT FURTHER

More about sin on page 109.

8 ¦ Remember God

Here's some more guidance on how God wants His people to live. Once again, remembering Him is at the heart of it all.

👁 **Read Exodus 20 v 7**

ENGAGE YOUR BRAIN

▶ *Why is God's 'name' so important?*

We've already seen how God's name told the Israelites about His character — who He was. To misuse it or treat it lightly shows contempt for who He is.

GET ON WITH IT

Hopefully it shocks you or makes you uncomfortable when friends or family use Jesus' name as a swear word. Can you think of something to say that shows how offensive it is to you without sounding judgmental?

👁 **Read verses 8–11**

▶ *What should the Sabbath be like? (v9–10)*

▶ *Why is the Sabbath special? (v11)*

Interestingly the command about the Sabbath isn't repeated in the New Testament, but while not all Christians believe we have to have a special day as the Jews did, the principle to have a day of rest and time to meet with other Christians is still a good one.

▶ *Do you work hard?*

▶ *Do you get enough rest?*

▶ *Are you making meeting other believers a priority?*

TALK IT OVER

Why is it so important for Christians to meet together regularly? Chat it through with an older Christian — look at Hebrews 10 v 24–25 as a starting point.

THE BOTTOM LINE

Remember God.

➡ **TAKE IT FURTHER**

Take a break on page 109.

9 | The final six

**God's top ten countdown is nearing its end.
More of the big ten now...**

 Read Exodus 20 v 12–17

ENGAGE YOUR BRAIN

God's blueprint for how His people were to live covers thoughts, words and deeds.

▷ *Can you spot examples of each in these verses?*

▷ *Do you think Christians have to obey the Ten Commandments today?*

Remember that the Israelites had already been rescued by God. The Ten Commandments and all the other laws that followed were to help them live after they had been rescued. So for us, following these or any other rules won't get us into God's good books — it's trusting Jesus that rescues us. In fact the Ten Commandments often show up how rubbish we are and how much we need the rescue that Jesus offers.

But Jesus didn't abolish these commands, so they are not irrelevant — in fact He took them even further. Take a few moments to read **Matthew 5 v 17–48**.

▷ *What have the Ten Commandments taught you about God?*

PRAY ABOUT IT

Have these commands of God highlighted any areas of your life where you're not pleasing Him? Pray about that now.

THE BOTTOM LINE

God wants to be God of our thoughts, words and actions.

➡ TAKE IT FURTHER

A little more on page 109.

10 | Powerful God

God has laid out the first part of His blueprint for how His people should live — so how will they respond?

👁 **Read Exodus 20 v 18–21**

ENGAGE YOUR BRAIN

▷ *What is the Israelites' reaction to what they have seen and heard? (v18–19)*

▷ *What do verses 18, 19 and 21 remind us about God?*

▷ *And about human beings?*

Remind yourself of the end of chapter 19 — to come face to face with God (or anywhere remotely near Him) is a terrifying experience. His holiness shows up our sin. When Peter witnessed one of Jesus' first miracles he cried: *'Go away from me, Lord; I am a sinful man!'* (Luke 5 v 8)

PRAY ABOUT IT

Do you sometimes forget how holy and awesomely powerful God is? Spend some time reflecting on that now. Then thank Him that we can speak to Him with confidence

because of what Jesus accomplished on the cross.

👁 **Read verses 22–26**

▷ *What made the Israelites uniquely privileged? (v22)*

▷ *So what does God remind them about? (v23)*

God then gives them some instructions about how they can approach Him. The simple altar meant anyone could make a sacrifice to God to have their sins forgiven, BUT they mustn't get too close (v26) without being properly prepared (more on this later).

THE BOTTOM LINE

God is perfect and holy and deserves our full respect and worship.

➡ **TAKE IT FURTHER**

More about this on page 109.

11 | Serving servants

After the big picture of the Ten Commandments come a whole load of detailed guidelines for how Israel was to live. It seems strange that the first one deals with slavery — surely God has just rescued His people out of slavery!

👁 Read Exodus 21 v 1–11

ENGAGE YOUR BRAIN

▷ *How long could a master keep a slave? (v2)*

When we think of slavery we probably have all kinds of negative images, like the plantations in North America in the 19th century, or the disgusting human trafficking which goes on around the world today. But Israelite slaves were more like paid servants who had to be loyal to one family rather than being able to quit whenever they felt like it.

▷ *Can you sum up in a word the manner in which slaves should be treated?*

God makes it clear that the way one Israelite treats another, even if he or she is a slave, should be very different from how they had been mistreated by the Egyptians.

▷ *How were female slaves different from male slaves? (v7-11)*

As women could be particularly vulnerable, there were special instructions to protect female slaves — they were not to be sold to foreigners (v8) and if she was married to the owner's son she became his daughter and was to be treated with respect, even if the son married again (v10).

PRAY ABOUT IT

We might not always like or understand what we read in the Bible. Ask God to help you have His perspective on life.

THE BOTTOM LINE

Treat others as you would like to be treated.

→ TAKE IT FURTHER

More about slavery on page 110.

12 | Revenge isn't sweet

On to the serious stuff now — accidental death, murder, fights etc. God recognises that despite His commands not to behave badly, these kinds of things will happen. So what follows is how to deal with them.

👁 Read Exodus 21 v 12–36

ENGAGE YOUR BRAIN

▷ What two categories of injuries are dealt with in these verses?

▷ What is the underlying principle for handling all of these incidents? (v23–25)

▷ With the Ten Commandments in mind, skim through these verses and make a note of how these events link to some of the commandments:

▷ Look at verses 23–25. Do they seem fair to you?

The idea of an eye for an eye is quite attractive to us — you slapped me so I'll slap you. You spoke about me behind my back, so I'll spread a bit of gossip about you. But the whole point of the law was to limit revenge from going too far, not to encourage it.

▷ Read what Jesus has to say in Matthew 5 v 38–42.

PRAY ABOUT IT

Ask for God's help to follow Jesus' example:
'Christ suffered for you, leaving you an example, that you should follow in his steps. "He committed no sin, and no deceit was found in his mouth." When they hurled their insults at him, he did not retaliate; when he suffered, he made no threats. Instead, he entrusted himself to him who judges justly.' (1 Peter 2 v 21–23)

THE BOTTOM LINE

Do not repay evil for evil.

➡ TAKE IT FURTHER

More revenge facts are on page 110.

ESSENTIAL

More than a book

In each issue of **engage** we'll take time out to explore a key truth about God, the Bible and Christianity. In Essential we gather together the teaching from the Bible on a particular subject, and try to explain it. This issue, we're looking at the Bible — can we trust it? What should we do with it?

Important question: How do we know what God is like?

You can look up at the stars and know He's big — must be if He made all that. You can look at a sunset and know He's wildly creative. You can look at a duck-billed platypus and know He has a sense of humour. But looking at what someone has made can only take you so far. To find out how someone thinks, and what they want — what they're really like — you have to hear them speak.

And that's what's special about this ancient and, at times, weirdly obscure collection of 66 books that make up the Bible. It is God speaking to you.

INSPIRED WORDS

Even though it was written by people, the Bible is made up of God's words. Every bit of Scripture is 'God-breathed' (2 Timothy 3 v 16). That doesn't mean that God dictated the Scriptures one syllable at a time but it does mean that the Holy Spirit closely guided the authors of the various books and ensured that what we have in our hands are God's thoughts — not just human opinions. That's why we call it God's word.

TRUE WORDS

And because God cannot lie (Titus 1 v 2), we can be sure it is true. What the Bible says about God is right. What the Bible says about people is accurate (even though it might be uncomfortable at times!). What the Bible says about how we can become friends with God is not just a suggestion about how things might

work — God means what He says.

When John was writing his Gospel, he went as far as saying that God's word is 'truth' (John 17 v 17) — the very standard by which we measure whether everything else we see and hear is true or not.

And not just true back when the Bible was written, but true now. Because every single sentence has come from God, and God isn't boxed in by culture or time, they are true for all people in every age (1 Peter 1 v 25).

That's why Christians spend a lot of time and effort reading the Bible, hearing it, thinking about it, studying it and discussing it. It's God talking. It's so important to listen to Him and understand what He's saying.

REVEALING WORDS

Christians read the Bible because it is the ultimate way of knowing who God is, what He feels about us, what He wants from us and what the future holds. It's not a dry, dusty manual, but a love letter in which God pours out His heart to us. It's where God sets out what's really important for us to know about Him,

about ourselves, and about His plans for us and our world. It's where we discover what God has done for us in sending Jesus into the world as our Rescuer.

POWERFUL WORDS

God's words are words that impact our lives in the most breathtaking ways. They help us to change to be more like Jesus. Reading them is like surgery for the heart (Hebrews 4 v 12) — at times difficult, maybe even scary, but excitingly life-changing. Putting them into action is the best way to be equipped for living God's way (Ephesians 6 v 17) and to ensure that we will keep going in the faith and not give up (Matthew 4 v 4).

So much more than just a book — the Bible is a precious gift from God to inform us, equip us and change us. Ignoring the Bible is a dangerous business (James 1 v 22–24). It results in us thinking stuff about God and ourselves that just isn't right. So enjoy getting stuck into the word of God as often as possible. Have confidence that it's true and won't fail you. Ever.

Romans

Basic Christianity

Are you sitting comfortably? Well, you won't be for long because we're about to throw ourselves into one of the most in-your-face and challenging books in the Bible.

LIFE-CHANGING LETTER

Romans is actually a letter written by Paul around 60AD to Christians in Rome (centre of the world back then). Ordinary people like you and me. Paul didn't start the church there, but he would soon visit it.

Paul was the one chosen by Jesus to take the good news of the gospel to Gentiles (anyone who's not a Jew). Paul wants this Gentile church (though there were Jewish believers in it too) to grab hold of its responsibilities towards other members of God's people. In this case, to step outward to Jews — across a big fat cultural divide.

POWERFUL STUFF

Many people think *Romans* is the most important book they've ever read. Some have come to trust in Jesus for the first time after reading it. Some are stunned by its amazing truths about God and about people. Some find their faith shaken to life like never before.

Romans may be a hard read at times, but it very clearly lays out the gospel — the basic truths of Christianity. All the stuff we need to get our heads around. And it slaps down the implications of believing it and living as a Christian.

Be careful, this book could change your life...

13 | Dear Romans...

When people write letters, they usually begin: 'Dear Bob...' and don't sign their name until the end. But Paul's style is different. In fact, he gets completely distracted by something else during his introduction.

👁 Read Romans 1 v 1–7

ENGAGE YOUR BRAIN

▷ *How does Paul introduce himself? (v1)*

▷ *What and who does Paul go off on a tangent about? (v2–4)*

▷ *What facts are we told about Jesus? (v3–4)*

Paul was God's specially chosen apostle, sent out by God to tell people the truth about Jesus. He was 'set apart' to spread the gospel — the good news about Jesus —which is what he gets so excited about.

Paul wants everyone to hear the gospel that was promised by Old Testament prophets. It was fulfilled in Jesus — God's Son, who became human, to die and be raised back to life through the power of the Holy Spirit. But how does all that affect us?

👁 Read verses 5–7 again

▷ *How does Paul describe his job? (v5)*

▷ *What does faith in Jesus lead to? (end of v5)*

▷ *How does he describe the Christians in Rome? (v6–7)*

Paul was sent to call ordinary Christians (some Jewish, but mostly Gentiles) to believe in and obey Jesus Christ. The guys he was writing to belonged to Jesus. And so do you if you've put your trust in Him. In fact, if you're a Christian, you are *'loved by God'* and can be called a saint! (v7)

PRAY ABOUT IT

Ask God to show you the whole truth of the gospel as you read Romans. Ask Him to use this book to change your life, building up your faith and making you more obedient to Him.

THE BOTTOM LINE

The gospel makes saints — people set apart to live for God.

➔ TAKE IT FURTHER

More great truths on page 110.

The power of God

Do you ever pray for Christians overseas who you've never met? Paul was doing the same, and encouraging them too. And he also had some more challenging words about the gospel.

👁 Read Romans 1 v 8–13

ENGAGE YOUR BRAIN

▷ What was Paul thankful to God for? (v8)

▷ Even though he'd yet to meet them, what did Paul do? (v9–10)

▷ Why did Paul want to visit Rome? (v11–13)

The faith of these Christians in Rome had become big news (v8). So much so that Paul regularly prayed for them and longed to visit them and help strengthen them in their faith (v12). So that even more people in Rome would become Christ-followers.

PRAY ABOUT IT

▷ Which faraway Christians can you pray for?
Go on then — do it!

▷ Have you ever thought of visiting them or writing/emailing to encourage them?

👁 Read verses 14-17

▷ How does Paul describe his commitment to spreading the gospel? (v14–15)

▷ Why shouldn't we be ashamed of the gospel? (v16)

Paul is passionate about sharing Jesus with people, whatever their background (v14). We shouldn't be ashamed of the gospel — it is the power of God to save people! And Christians have a duty to share what God has entrusted to them.

SHARE IT

▷ How do these verses make you think differently about sharing the gospel?

▷ Who can you talk to about Jesus, who you wouldn't normally consider?

→ TAKE IT FURTHER
More good news on page 110.

15 | No excuses

Paul says that the truth about Jesus — the gospel — is the power of God to save those who believe. Save them from what?

👁 Read Romans 1 v 18–20

ENGAGE YOUR BRAIN

▷ *Why is God angry with human beings? (v18–19)*

▷ *What's one way we know God exists? (v20)*

▷ *Why should we know better than to walk out on God? (v20)*

People need saving from God's wrath — His anger and punishment for rejecting Him. Paul says that no one has an excuse for not believing in God or living for Him (see *Tricky* on page 36). Nature screams at us that God exists and shows us how powerful and perfect He is (v20). But people still live as if God isn't there.

👁 Read verses 21–23

▷ *What is God particularly angry about? (v21)*

▷ *Does anyone have an excuse for disobeying God?*

This is serious stuff. Sadly, many people refuse to admit that God exists, even though they know it deep down. Or they admit His existence but refuse to let Him rule their lives or give Him the glory and thanks He deserves as their powerful Creator. In fact, people will worship anything rather than God (v23).

PRAY ABOUT IT

▷ *Who do you know who refuses to trust in God?*
▷ *What about yourself?*

Spend a longer time than usual bringing these people before God in prayer. Plead with Him to change them and forgive them.

THE BOTTOM LINE
There's no excuse for rejecting God.

➡ TAKE IT FURTHER
Revealing stuff on page 111.

16 | Trampling truth

More tough stuff today. Yesterday we discovered that no one has an excuse for rejecting God. Today, Paul tells us that God is already punishing people who go their own way, shunning Him.

👁 Read Romans 1 v 24–27

ENGAGE YOUR BRAIN

▷ *What has God 'given us over to' for rejecting Him? (v24)*

▷ *Why is it so dumb to worship anything other than God? (v25)*

▷ *What does Paul say about homosexuality? (v26–27)*

God is already revealing His anger at those who reject Him — by allowing them to sin. People want to ignore Him and do whatever they want. So God lets them. But people are living a lie if they think it's better than serving God (v25). Paul says that rejecting God leads to abuse of sex, homosexual relationships (more about that in *Take it further*) and social breakdown.

👁 Read verses 28–32

▷ *What do people know about God? (v32)*

▷ *But what is their response? (v32)*

Deep down, people know that God exists and will punish sin, but they bury these facts and ignore them. They reject Him. So God is right to be angry with them and punish them.

None of us has lived up to what we know about God — we've deliberately kicked Him out of our lives. We can't plead ignorance or make excuses either. God's not an idle spectator, overlooking His world, happily letting evil continue. He's expressing His anger for all to see, and one day He'll carry out a final judgment. See why we need Jesus?

PRAY ABOUT IT

Talk openly with God about how today's bit of Romans has made you feel. Say sorry. Thank Him for sending Jesus to rescue us from sin.

→ TAKE IT FURTHER

More about gay issues on page 111.

17 Passing judgment

"Did you hear what Sasha did? Unbelievable — none of us would have done it." Almost without realising it, we can point an accusing finger at people. But God's finger is more accurate than ours.

👁 Read Romans 2 v 1–4

ENGAGE YOUR BRAIN

▷ *What's the problem with judging others? (v3)*

▷ *What do people fail to realise about God? (v4)*

We all think we're on the 'good' side and look down our noses at others and their sin. But none of us are sinless — we're just as bad. None of us have the right to criticise others. Only God judges fairly, seeing all the facts (v2).

👁 Read verses 5–11

▷ *How would you describe God's anger and punishment in v5–6?*

▷ *How do v8–9 make you feel?*

▷ *And how about v7 and v10?*

If we fail to admit we've sinned against God, then we're storing up God's wrath (v5). We can't hide behind claims of being good. God is completely fair and will judge everyone as they deserve (v6). That includes rewarding everyone who **always** does good and pleases God. But who lives like that? No one!

THINK IT OVER

▷ *Who do you criticise harshly?*

▷ *What will you do about that?*

▷ *Know anyone who thinks their Christian upbringing or good behaviour means they're all right with God?*

PRAY ABOUT IT

Talk honestly with God about your answers to these questions.

THE BOTTOM LINE
Only God judges fairly.

→ TAKE IT FURTHER

More accusations on page 111.

18 Justice for all

It must be tricky being a judge, wondering if the sentence you've just dished out is fair or not. Paul says even though we get things wrong sometimes, God doesn't. He's the perfect, totally fair judge who doesn't show favouritism.

Read Romans 2 v 12–16

Slowly. It's difficult stuff.

ENGAGE YOUR BRAIN

These Jews had grown up being taught God's law and knew it well.

▶ *Why wasn't knowing God's law enough? (v13)*

God's judgment will be absolutely fair. Paul says whether you're a Jew or a Gentile, **everyone** has sinned against God and we'll all face His judgment.

We're a lot like the Jewish people Paul mentions, because we have God's law in the Bible. That is a great privilege compared to parts of the world where hardly anyone has a Bible. But, because we have the Bible, which tells us clearly what's right and wrong, we have **no excuse** when we disobey God.

People who don't have the Bible are like the Gentiles Paul talks about.

But God's law is written on their hearts (v15). Their conscience tells them what's right or wrong. They too have no excuse. **Everyone** has broken God's law and deserves to be punished.

▶ *Who will judge everyone? (v16)*

Whether or not God punishes us depends on our reaction to Jesus. If we accept Him, He'll rescue us as our Saviour. If we reject Him, He'll condemn us as our Judge. Tough but fair.

PRAY ABOUT IT

Talk honestly with God about where you're at and your response to Jesus. And pray for friends who think they're good enough, yet refuse to accept Jesus.

THE BOTTOM LINE

God will judge everyone fairly.

➔ TAKE IT FURTHER

Just desserts on page 111.

19 Practise what you preach

"Josh is always talking behind people's backs; only yesterday I heard him say..."
Does hypocrisy get on your nerves?
God hates double standards too.

Read Romans 2 v 17–24

ENGAGE YOUR BRAIN

▶ *What's Paul criticism of these over-confident Jews? (v21)*

▶ *What's the terrible result of their actions? (v24)*

It's dangerous to focus on other people's faults — we end up missing our own. These Jews were so confident that they were right with God and were top dogs that they looked down on others. They were blind to their own double standards.

Read verses 25–29

Circumcision was a sign of being one of God's people. Jewish men were proud of being circumcised, of being God's chosen people.

▶ *Would it protect them from God's anger? (v25)*

▶ *What does God look for in a person? (v29)*

Being Jewish or being circumcised (or having Christian parents) was not enough to put you right with God. These Jews had nothing to be smug about. God isn't interested in what a person is like on the outside. It's all about your heart being devoted to Him; living your life God's way.

THINK IT OVER

▶ *Do you think you deserve preferential treatment from God?*

▶ *Do you ever congratulate yourself for being 'good'?*

▶ *Are you practising what you preach?*

PRAY ABOUT IT

Ask God to help you practise what you preach, so that you don't just look like a Christian on Sundays, but devote your whole life to Him.

➔ TAKE IT FURTHER

A little more can be found on page 111.

20 | What's the point?

It seems as if Paul's been saying there was no advantage in being one of God's chosen people — the Jews. But he wasn't saying that at all. Check out Paul arguing with himself!

👁 Read Romans 3 v 1–4

ENGAGE YOUR BRAIN

▶ *Is there any advantage in being Jewish? (v2)*

▶ *Does God's ability to keep His promises rely on His people having faith in Him? (v4)*

A great privilege of being Jewish was that they'd been given God's own words (the Old Testament). But a privilege can do nothing for you if you abuse it. It's the same for people brought up in a Christian home — they get taught about Jesus from a young age. But if they refuse to follow Jesus, they only have themselves to blame.

Paul says: Don't think that because some Jews have no faith in Jesus, God has broken His promises. God's faithfulness is never in doubt, even if that makes everyone else a liar. God always keeps His promises.

👁 Read verses 5–8

▶ *Our sin shows how holy and forgiving God is. Isn't God being unfair to punish us for it? (v6)*

▶ *Isn't our sinfulness doing God a favour? Can't we just carry on sinning? (end of v8)*

Paul barely answers these questions. It's so ridiculous to suggest that God is unfair or that it's OK for us to keep sinning against Him that Paul dismisses these arguments. God is perfect, holy and totally fair. People who reject God deserve His punishment. End of story.

PRAY ABOUT IT

Ask God to help you be more like Paul — to know your Bible well so that you can answer people's arguments against God and His Word.

→ TAKE IT FURTHER

For more on God's justice, try page 111.

21 No one's perfect

I expect you've had no problem following all of Paul's ideas and arguments in Romans so far. In fact, I bet you could sum it all up in one sentence. No? Me neither. We'd best let Paul sum it all up...

👁 Read Romans 3 v 9–18

ENGAGE YOUR BRAIN

▷ *What big point is Paul making with all these Old Testament quotes? (v10–18)*

▷ *What are humans naturally like according to these verses?*

▷ *Any exceptions?*

Have you got the message? NO ONE is sinless. NO ONE is good enough for God. We've all turned away from Him and sin can be found in every part of our lives. There are no exceptions.

👁 Read verses 19–20

▷ *Can we say anything to God to defend ourselves? (v19)*

▷ *Who is good enough for God? (v20)*

I may think I live a good life or am a better person than other people I know, but that counts for nothing.

NO ONE meets God's perfect standards. None of us can say anything to excuse us from the punishment we deserve. Which is exactly the point God's law wants designed to get us to.

Don't worry, that's not the end of the story — there's good news tomorrow.

SHARE IT

▷ *When you talk about Christianity, do you water down or miss out bits about sin and punishment?*

▷ *How vital is it to understand that we're all guilty before God?*

▷ *So how will you talk about these things with friends?*

PRAY ABOUT IT

Talk to God about these issues and ask Him to help you be honest but sensitive with your friends.

→ TAKE IT FURTHER

More heavy stuff on page 112.

22 | God's free gift

We've all sinned and deserve God's punishment. No one is good enough for God. That's devastating news but it's not the end of the story. Now read what some people say is the most important paragraph ever written...

👁 Read Romans 3 v 21–26

ENGAGE YOUR BRAIN

Now read it again verse by verse and we'll unpack Paul's incredible words. You won't read anything like this outside of the Bible.

v21 None of us can keep God's perfect law. So He's made a way for us to be put right with Him.

v22 It's not based on how good we are. We can only be made right with God by relying on Jesus and what He's done for us.

v23 There's no difference between Jew or Gentile or anyone. We've all rejected God and all deserve His punishment.

v24 So we don't deserve God's forgiveness, but He offers it to us anyway. It's a free gift. That's **grace**. Because of Jesus, we can be *justified* — forgiven; just as if I'd never sinned. Christians have

been *redeemed* — bought back by Jesus.

v25 God sent His Son to die to take away God's anger against us. But we've got to trust in Jesus.

v26 Through Jesus, we see God's perfect justice and incredible patience with sinners like us.

THINK IT OVER

▷ *Summarise the good news from these verses in your own words.*
▷ *What does Jesus' death tell us about God?*

SHARE IT

How can you use the ideas in this mind-blowing passage to tell your mates about what God has done for sinful people like us? Take time to work out how you can clearly explain this great news. Write it down. Practise it. And then do it.

➡ TAKE IT FURTHER

More great news on page 112.

23 Faith the facts

Paul sounds a bit schizophrenic, having this conversation with himself. But he's answering some really important questions and concerns that Jews had about the gospel.

👁 Read Romans 3 v 27–28

ENGAGE YOUR BRAIN

▷ *Could Jews boast about being God's special people? (v27)*

▷ *Can we boast about being God's people, Christians?*

▷ *Why not?*

No one can boast about being chosen by God — we haven't earned it by living good lives. It's a free gift, achieved by Jesus dying on the cross for us. We've got nothing to be proud about — Jesus did all the hard work! We just have to trust in Him.

👁 Read verses 29–30

▷ *Who is the gospel for?*

The great news is that God offers forgiveness to EVERYONE, whatever their background. There is only one God, and there's only one way to be put right with God: faith in Jesus. And that's true for everyone.

👁 Read verse 31

If faith in Jesus is the only way to God, was God's law pointless? Absolutely not! By trusting in Jesus, we become what God's law wants us to be but can't make us.

The law shows it's impossible for us to please God, and so urges us to trust in Jesus. But because of what Jesus has done, God will accept us as perfect law-keepers! Amazing. And it's all down to Jesus.

PRAY ABOUT IT

Ask God to help you...
- not be proud about your faith or look down on others
- share the gospel with other people; it's good news for everyone
- live God's way, not your own.

→ TAKE IT FURTHER

See what Jesus said about all this on page 112.

24 Faith works

Paul says that we're 'justified' (put right with God) by faith in Jesus; not by doing good works. He backs up his claims with two great Jewish heroes — Abraham and David.

👁 Read Romans 4 v 1–5

ENGAGE YOUR BRAIN

▷ *Was Abraham accepted by God because he worked hard and earned it?*

▷ *Does God only forgive 'good' people? (v5)*

Many people believe that if they live good lives they'll be accepted by God. But we're **all** sinful and are not good enough for God — even Abraham, the Jews' hero. God accepted Abraham (in fact, treated him as righteous), not because he lived a good life, but because he believed God. Trusted in Him.

Incredibly, God justifies (forgives) wicked people if they trust in Him to save them (v5). How awesome is that?

👁 Read verses 6–8

▷ *How good did King David feel when he wrote this?*

▷ *What's the great news for believers? (v7–8)*

King David was so excited! God accepted Him even though he messed up many times. David trusted in God, so the Lord forgave his sins and would never hold them against Him. The same goes for anyone who trusts Jesus' death in their place to wipe out their sins.

PRAY ABOUT IT

If you truly mean it, admit to God that you're not good enough to be with Him. Now thank God that if you trust in Jesus your sins are forgiven and God won't count them against you! Plenty to praise God for!

THE BOTTOM LINE

We're justified by faith, not works.

→ TAKE IT FURTHER

More info on faithful Abraham on page 112.

25 Showing promise

Is it just me, or do you find Paul's letter to Christians in Rome tricky to understand? It's brain-achingly hard at times, but it's vital truth about Christianity. So stick with it — it's worth it.

👁 Read Romans 4 v 9–12

ENGAGE YOUR BRAIN

▷ When was Abraham counted righteous (right with God)? (v10)

▷ So, who is Abraham the 'father' of? (v11–12)

This was really controversial at the time. Most Jews couldn't cope with the idea that they weren't the only ones special and acceptable to God. Paul says being circumcised and being Jewish doesn't make you right with God. Abe was circumcised as a sign to show that he belonged to God — it didn't make him right with God.

👁 Read verses 13–17

▷ Did God make great promises to Abraham because of his law-keeping or his faith? (v13)

▷ So who is God's promise to — only Jews or all believers? (v16)

God's promises to Abraham can be found in Genesis 12 v 1–3. God didn't make these promises because Abraham obeyed His law. It was because of Abe's faith in God.

God's promise to Abraham is for **all believers**. He promised that Abraham would be the father of many nations. That promise means that anyone can be part of God's people, not just the Jews. We don't deserve to be God's people — it's an undeserved gift. Grace.

PRAY ABOUT IT

Thank God that we don't have to earn His love and forgiveness. Thank Him that it's a gift to anyone who accepts it. Pray for people you know who haven't accepted God's gift.

➡ TAKE IT FURTHER

Wise words from Jesus on page 113.

26 Credit note

'We'll win this match!' promises your coach. But you're losing badly, half your team is injured and the opposition is HUGE! Would you believe his promise? Abraham had an even harder promise to believe.

Read Romans 4 v 18–22

ENGAGE YOUR BRAIN

▷ *Why did God's promise that Abraham would have many children seem so unlikely? (v19)*

▷ *How would you describe Abraham's faith in God? (v20-21)*

God promised Abraham millions of offspring. But Abe was 100 years old and his wife was unable to have kids. Yet Abraham still believed God's promise against all the odds. So he was counted 'righteous' — right with God.

True faith in God realises that nothing is impossible for God. He keeps His promises. Even when all hope is lost. Faith rests entirely on what God has promised, not on what we do.

Read verses 23–25

▷ *What's God's promise for those who trust in Jesus? (v24–25)*

We deserve to be condemned to eternal death for rejecting God. Instead, God sent Jesus to die in our place and then raised Him from death, providing a rescue for everyone who has faith in Him. Those of us who believe will be counted as right with God. Phenomenal.

GET ON WITH IT

Learn verse 25 by heart. This is an incredible truth that all Christians can hold on to. The resurrection is proof that Jesus has paid for our sins.

PRAY ABOUT IT

Thank God that He keeps His promises. Thank Him for His promise to put us right with Him.

THE BOTTOM LINE

Have faith in God who keeps His promises.

→ TAKE IT FURTHER

A recap on the first four chapters of Romans is on page 113.

27 Peace and joy

Paul says we're 'justified by faith' — we're declared right with God as we trust in Jesus' death on the cross. We won't be condemned by God as we deserve to be. Now Paul tells us that more goodies are coming our way.

👁 **Read Romans 5 v 1–2**

ENGAGE YOUR BRAIN

▷ *What do people who trust in Jesus now have? (v1)*

The problem
God is rightly angry with our sin against Him. We deserve to be punished.

The solution
'We have been justified by faith' — Jesus took God's anger and punishment on Himself for everyone who has faith in His death for sinners.

The result
'We have peace with God through our Lord Jesus Christ.' God's anger has been dealt with by Jesus, so Christians have peace with God.

What a sensational result! God at peace with believers — for ever. Even their sin can't alter that, since Jesus has already taken God's punishment for it.

👁 **Read verses 1–2 again**

▷ *What else have believers gained? (v2)*

▷ *What should be their response?*

Having faith in Jesus is like a door that lets you into the great room full of God's blessing ('grace'). Sin was the barrier stopping us getting in, but now we have full access to it. And that should fill us with great joy.

PRAY ABOUT IT

Think about God's grace — all He's done for you and given you. Praise Him for specific things. Thank Him. Tell Him how it makes you feel.

THE BOTTOM LINE

Faith in Jesus gives us peace with God.

→ **TAKE IT FURTHER**

Peacefully turn to page 113.

28 | No pain, no gain

We've been reading about Jesus' death in our place and how it puts believers right with God. But we're not just passive observers of Jesus' suffering — Christians can expect to share in it too.

◉ Read Romans 5 v 3–5

ENGAGE YOUR BRAIN

▷ What surprising thing can Christians get excited about? (v3)

▷ Why should we be happy to suffer? (v3–5)

Jesus suffered and died to save us. Suffering for being a Christian comes with the territory. We're promised that people will persecute us. But why would we be happy about it???

Paul tells us that we should see the difficulties of life opportunities to grow spiritually. God has a great plan for our lives but it doesn't guarantee an easy, relaxing life.

Instead, God allows us to face times of suffering which make us trust in Him more, and help us grow in spiritual character. 'Suffering produces perseverance; perseverance, character; and character, hope.' God allows us to experience hard times so that we develop spiritual muscles, and are made more fit to serve Him.

And that really is something to celebrate, especially as we have the certain hope of sharing God's glory. And the Holy Spirit in us reminds us of God's overwhelming love for us (v5). The Christian life really is a matter of 'no pain, no gain'. Let's look at our troubles as opportunities to learn and grow spiritually.

TALK IT THROUGH

Think about hard times you've faced. Can you see God at work in those situations, making you stronger?

PRAY ABOUT IT

Ask God to help you through any tough situations you face. Ask Him to help you not give up. Thank Him that He's with you, building you up along the way. Thank Him for the certain hope of eternal life.

→ TAKE IT FURTHER

More pain on page 113.

29 | Unbeatable love

Does God love you?
Do you genuinely feel that He does?
Is there any evidence that God loves you?

👁 **Read Romans 5 v 6–8**

ENGAGE YOUR BRAIN

▷ How does God show His love for us? (v8)

▷ How would you describe God's timing? (v6)

Simple. We know God loves us because His own Son Jesus died for us. While we were still God's enemies. And God's given His Spirit to all who trust Him.

You may have read stories of people giving their own lives to save loved ones. But God's love shown on the cross beats all human love hands down. We were God's enemies, sinning against Him when He gave His Son to die in our place.

👁 **Read verses 9–11**
Verse 9 talks of the final day when God will judge His world

▷ What's true for those who trust in Jesus? (v9)

▷ Why can we be sure of this? (v10)

If God's done the difficult thing (v10a), of course we can be sure He'll complete the job and hold on to us when His judgment comes (v10b). And there's even more to get excited about (v11).

PRAY ABOUT IT
Will you praise and thank God for what He's done? Spend time thanking Him for sending His Son Jesus to die for sinners like yourself.

THE BOTTOM LINE
While we were still sinners, Christ died for us.

➡ **TAKE IT FURTHER**
Positive thinking on page 113.

No excuses

Each issue in TRICKY, we tackle those mind-bendingly difficult questions that confuse us all, as well as questions that friends bombard us with to catch us out. This time: **What happens to people who've never heard the gospel?**

Imagine the scene. You've spent ages planning your costume and the day's arrived. You get dressed up, paint your face, put on the comedy wig and set off for the party. Then you ring the doorbell only to find it answered by your best mate and a roomful of friends... none of them are in fancy dress. Aaaargh! Total embarrassment and humiliation, all because you hadn't heard that there'd been a change of plan.

But what about those who haven't heard the gospel? What will be the consequences for those people? Well, the Bible gives three answers.

1. EVERYONE HAS HEARD SOMETHING

Romans 1 v 18–20 is very clear about this: *'What may be known about God is plain to them, because God has made it plain to them. For since the creation of the world God's invisible qualities — his eternal power and divine nature — have been clearly seen, being understood from what has been made, so that men are without excuse.'*

Everyone can see evidence for God in the awesome world He created. The problem is that people would rather not admit it — they suppress the truth (v18).

Sadly, many people refuse to admit that God exists, even though they know it deep down. Or they admit His existence but refuse to let Him rule their lives. All human beings face God's anger because by nature we ignore Him.

> Everyone can see evidence for God in the awesome world He created.

2. GOD IS LOVING AND FAIR

What about the friend who's just lost a baby cousin, a kid that never got the chance to hear the gospel? How will God treat that baby?

Firstly, we know that God is compassionate and slow to anger (Exodus 34 v 6–7) and secondly, we know that He is totally just — we are all judged according to what we have done (Romans 2 v 6). We know we can trust Him to act fairly and can safely leave these difficult cases in His hands (Acts 17 v 31). God doesn't want anyone to perish (2 Peter 3 v 9).

But while we know we can trust God to always do what's right, we also know that believing the gospel guarantees that people will be saved. That's why we should support the work of people sharing the gospel in countries where there are hardly any Christians — both in prayer and with money if we're able.

3. FOCUS ON THOSE AROUND YOU

This is the real heart of the matter for us. We have heard the gospel — in fact, many of our friends and family who don't yet trust in Jesus have also heard the gospel. We live in countries where there are churches on every corner, where many homes have a Bible somewhere in them, where there are Christians in pretty much every school, college and workplace.

When answering a similar question, Jesus told the questioners to stop worrying about these other people, and concentrate on themselves — *read Luke 13 v 1–5.*

Let's not kid ourselves, the consequences of ignoring and rejecting God are severe. But thankfully, Jesus offers us a way out — He died to rescue us from the consequences of our rebellion against God.

So if you haven't yet repented — turned away from ignoring God — and believed in Jesus, then do it now! And if you have, keep sharing that saving message with others! Stick at it, keep praying, keep speaking and ask God to open people's eyes to the truth of the gospel.

Luke

Jesus: the early years

Ever had a friend tell you that something unbelievable happened? Maybe a huge celeb shopping in the local mall. It's so outrageous, you don't believe a word of it until you see it in the local paper and a friend tells you they saw it with their own eyes.

CHECK THE EVIDENCE

There have been some outrageous claims about Jesus — His mother was a virgin; He could do miracles; He raised people back to life; He was God's Son. Without proof, we can easily ignore these claims. What we need is someone who was actually around at the time, and that's where Luke steps in.

DOCTOR DO-LOTS

Luke was a well-educated doctor, and a mate of Paul. He did his own investigation into the claims about Jesus and even checked if all the stuff the Old Testament prophets claimed about the Christ came true in Jesus (it did). He then compiled all his findings into 'an orderly account' and sent it to his friend Theophilus, to convince him of the truth about Jesus.

PUBLIC INQUIRY

In this issue of Engage, we start with Jesus' early years and see how God was working in an incredible way right from the start.

Explore all the evidence and make up your own mind about Jesus.

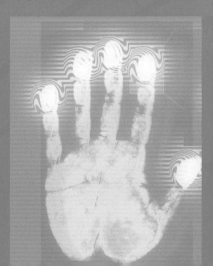

30 | Dumbstruck

It's a flying start from Luke. He explains why he's writing this essay and then jumps straight into the story. Although Jesus doesn't get a mention just yet.

👁 Read Luke 1 v 1–4

ENGAGE YOUR BRAIN

▷ *Why did Luke do this investigation and write this account? (v4)*

👁 Read verses 5–17

▷ *Why was the angel's news so surprising? (v7, v13)*

▷ *What would John be like? (v14–15)*

▷ *And what would he do? (v16–17)*

This couple were elderly and had given up on having kids, but God had other plans. Their son would become a great and godly man who would bring many Jews back to serving God. He would make them ready for King Jesus.

👁 Read verses 18–25

▷ *Why was Zechariah struck dumb? (v20)*

▷ *How did Elizabeth react differently? (v25)*

Unsurprisingly, Zechariah was surprised by the shock news and questioned Gabriel. So God's angel struck him dumb until birth-day. This reminds us just how seriously we should take God's word. It's not to be taken lightly, but to be believed and treasured and allowed to change our lives.

GET ON WITH IT

▷ *What can you do to make sure you take seriously what you read in the Bible?*

▷ *How can you treasure God's word as Elizabeth did?*

PRAY ABOUT IT

Thank God that He works in people's lives in astonishing ways. Ask Him to change your attitude to His word.

→ TAKE IT FURTHER

History lesson on page 113.

39

31 | Pregnant pause

It's time for part two of 'Gabriel's Surprise Visits'. The scene is a house in the town of Nazareth. Get ready to see another jaw drop and hit the floor in shock.

👁 Read Luke 1 v 26–33

ENGANGE YOUR BRAIN

▷ *What jaw-dropping promises did Gabriel make about Jesus?*

He will be...

He'll be called...

The Lord will...

And He will...

His kingdom...

Out of the blue, God's messenger told a young virgin that she was pregnant and her unborn baby would be called God's Son and would rule the Jews forever. What a shock.

👁 Read verses 34–38

▷ *How could young virgin Mary be pregnant? (v35)*

▷ *What great truth does Mary learn about God? (v37)*

▷ *What's Mary's response? (v38)*

We're not told exactly how this virgin could have a baby. All we need to know is that 'Nothing is impossible with God'. Nothing at all. Mary believes God can do the impossible and is prepared for God to use her as His servant.

THINK IT OVER

▷ *Do you truly believe that nothing's impossible for God?*

▷ *What do you find hard to believe God can do?*

▷ *How can you serve Him more willingly?*

PRAY ABOUT IT
Talk to God openly about this stuff.

THE BOTTOM LINE
Nothing is impossible with God.

TAKE IT FURTHER
Pause for a while on page 114.

32 Bump jump

Can you remember being really excited about something when you were small? What was it? How did you show your excitement. Elizabeth's baby got excited about stuff before he was even born!

👁 Read Luke 1 v 39–45

ENGAGE YOUR BRAIN

▶ *How did Elizabeth know about her cousin's great news? (v41)*

Elizabeth was filled with the Holy Spirit and her baby jumped for joy when pregnant Mary turned up on her doorstep. God clearly showed Elizabeth (and John inside her!) that Mary would give birth to the Christ — the promised Rescuer.

👁 Read verses 46–56

▶ *How had God treated Mary? (v46–49)*

▶ *How had He treated His people (Israel)? (v50–55)*

▶ *What about His enemies? (v51–53)*

Mary realised what a privilege it was that God had chosen to use her to serve Him in this unbelievable way. God often uses unlikely, humble people in amazing ways (v48, v52). He shows mercy to all those who fear Him and serve Him (v50). He proved this to the Israelites by doing many *'mighty deeds'* for them and defeating their wealthy, proud enemies (v51–53).

God's plan to save His people didn't start with these two babies — it had been His plan all along: *'even as He said to our fathers'* (v56).

GET ON WITH IT

Try writing a poem or song or letter to God, like Mary's song (v46–56). Include things He's done specifically for you as well as for all Christians. Mention how it makes you feel. Don't hold back. Use it for your prayer time today.

➔ TAKE IT FURTHER

Jump to page 114 for more.

41

33 | Family fortunes

Mary (a virgin) is expecting a baby who will rule God's people for ever. Her elderly cousin Elizabeth is also pregnant with a special child and has a husband who's struck dumb for not believing an angel. Whatever next?

👁 Read Luke 1 v 57–66

ENGAGE YOUR BRAIN

▶ What did Elizabeth's neighbours recognise about what had happened? (v58)

▶ What effect did these events have on the local community? (v65–66)

When Zechariah showed he trusted God and gave his son the name John — as Gabriel had commanded — he got his voice back and immediately started praising God. Everyone was so flabbergasted by what had happened, the whole area was talking about it. They knew there was something special about John.

👁 Read verses 67–80

▶ What did Zechariah say about his son and what he'd do? (v76–79)

▶ What will God do for His people? (v69–75)

John would be God's messenger, a prophet. He'd prepare the way for Jesus — 'the horn of salvation' — who would rescue God's people from their biggest enemy, sin. He would bring forgiveness and guide all believers in the path of peace.

SHARE IT

Read the verses again and think how they could help you share with people what God has done for us by sending Jesus.

PRAY ABOUT IT

Zechariah's song reminds us what God was doing through Jesus — bringing a rescue. It reminds us of our deepest need — to have our sins forgiven. And it reminds us of the right response — living to please God.

THE BOTTOM LINE

Jesus is the great Rescuer.

➡ TAKE IT FURTHER

Promising stuff on page 114.

34 | Angel delight

You may have heard this story before. But try to see it with new eyes. As usual, Luke gives us the historical setting (v1–3) before he starts. Check out the excitement of the angels, the shepherds and the proud mum.

👁 **Read Luke 2 v 1–12**

ENGAGE YOUR BRAIN

▷ Who are the first to hear the great news? (v8–9)

▷ How does the angel describe the news? (v10)

▷ What two descriptions of Jesus does he give? (v11)

Not the first people you'd expect to hear the most impressive announcement ever. Regular shepherds out in the hills. But the angel gave them the most amazing **good news**, which would bring **great joy** to the world. It was news for **all people** — everyone needs to hear about Jesus.

Christ isn't Jesus' surname. It's a title. Like Messiah, it means 'anointed one' — God's chosen King. Following Jesus means accepting Him as King and Lord of your whole life.

👁 **Read verses 13–20**

▷ How did the shepherds react to this news? (v15–18, v20)

▷ What about Mary? (v19)

The angels praised God for sending His Son to bring peace to people on earth. Peace for those who trust in Him. The shepherds believed, and showed it by rushing to the maternity room and then telling everyone about it. Look at the effect it had — v18.

And look at Mary, taking in exactly how huge and important this was and how privileged she was.

PRAY ABOUT IT

Thank God for sending His Son personally as our Saviour. Recognise His right to run your life as Lord.

THE BOTTOM LINE

Jesus is the Saviour of the world.

➡ **TAKE IT FURTHER**

How to share the news — page 115.

35 | Simeon and Anna

Yesterday we saw how a bunch of ordinary shepherds were the first to hear the great news of Jesus' birth. Next to be let in on the news are two elderly temple workers.

👁 Read Luke 2 v 21–35

ENGAGE YOUR BRAIN

▷ What had God promised Simeon? (v26)

▷ How did Simeon describe Jesus? (v30–35)

▷ Who would Jesus save? (v31–32)

▷ What other effect would Jesus have on people? (v34–35)

Joseph and Mary took Jesus to the temple to offer sacrifices to God and vow that Jesus' life would be given to serving God. Simeon had been waiting his whole life to see the Christ — and here He was!

God showed Simeon who Jesus really was: the Saviour sent to rescue not just the Israelites, but Gentiles too (v31–32). But the message of Jesus isn't an easy one. He knows what's in our hearts (v35). Everyone who trusts Jesus' death to save them will 'rise' to eternal life. But those who reject Him will 'fall' to eternal death (v34).

👁 Read verses 36–40

▷ What was Anna's reaction to seeing who Jesus really is? (v38)

Anna spoke to people *'looking forward to the redemption of Jerusalem'* (v38) and Simeon was *'waiting for the consolation of Israel'* (v25). Israel, the people of God, needed to be comforted. But why?

It was about 400 years since the events at the end of the Old Testament. Israelites who trusted God were waiting for Him to bring His people back to Himself, as He'd promised. Simeon and Anna were shown by the Holy Spirit that Jesus was the one who would do it.

PRAY ABOUT IT

Using Simeon's words of praise (v29–32), make a list of things we can be thankful to God for. Add some things of your own too.

➡ TAKE IT FURTHER

Consolation? Redemption? Page 115.

36 | Missing Jesus

Today we look at the only event in Jesus' life between His birth and the age of 30 that's recorded in the Bible. Jesus' family were at the Passover feast in Jerusalem, celebrating God rescuing the Israelites from Egypt.

👁 Read Luke 2 v 41–52

ENGAGE YOUR BRAIN

▷ *Where had Jesus been for three days?*

▷ *What did His mother ask Him? (v48)*

▷ *How did Jesus describe where He'd been? (v49)*

▷ *What didn't they understand about His answer?*

▷ *What did Jesus do next? (v51–52)*

Understandably, Mary and Joseph were worried when their 12-year-old boy went missing. But Jesus was God's Son and spent the time in His Father's house (the temple), learning from Jewish teachers and asking them big questions. People were amazed at how much He understood.

At first, Jesus' answer to His mother sounds cheeky but later we're told that He obeyed His parents (v51) and that Jesus lived without sin (Hebrews 4 v 15). Yet even Joseph and Mary didn't fully grasp who He was (v50).

▷ *What does this Bible bit tell us about Jesus' identity?*

GET ON WITH IT

▷ *What specifically can you do to be more like Jesus?*

▷ *In what specific ways do you need to obey your parents more?*

PRAY ABOUT IT

Talk to God about these things.

→ TAKE IT FURTHER

Spend time with God — page 115.

37 ¦ Desert storm

Remember pregnant Elizabeth's bump jumping for joy when pregnant Mary come to visit? Well, the bumps have now both grown up and are about to make a huge impact on people's lives.

Read Luke 3 v 1–6

ENGAGE YOUR BRAIN

▷ What was John teaching? (v3)

▷ What did the prophet Isaiah say John would do? (v4–5)

▷ What would be the result? (v6)

John baptised people who 'repented' — turned away form their sinful way of living, turning back to God. John washed them in water as a sign of their repentance. Their sin would be 'washed away' and forgiven when Jesus died on the cross in their place. That's what John was preparing people for — Jesus, who would save mankind (v6).

Read verses 7–14

▷ How does John shatter the Jews' false confidence? (v8–9)

▷ How should people who've turned back to God live? (v11–14)

Their sins wouldn't be forgiven just because they were descended from Abraham. They had to turn their backs on sin. Jesus would die so that people's sins could be forgiven. And He would also return as Judge — everyone who hasn't turned to Him for forgiveness will be punished in hell (v9).

But people who have repented should live God's way. John gives three examples in v11–14.

GET ON WITH IT

What three specific things do you need to start doing or stop doing so you're living God's way?

1.

2.

3.

→ TAKE IT FURTHER

More stuff on page 115.

38 Burning question

John was making a big impact in the area. He preached that people needed to repent (turn back to God) and be baptised. But some people were confused about who he really was.

◉ Read Luke 3 v 15–20

ENGAGE YOUR BRAIN

▷ *Who did people think John might be? (v15)*

▷ *How did John answer them? (v16)*

▷ *How does John describe Jesus, the Christ? (v16–17)*

▷ *What do you think v17 means?*

Some people thought John might be the Christ — the King who God had promised would rescue His people. But John spoke of *'one more powerful'* (Jesus), who would give people the Holy Spirit to help them live God's way.

The Christ would also come with *fire*. Verse 17 uses the picture of harvest time — gathering good crops and burning the bad stuff. Jesus will judge people — gathering those who trust in Him, but punishing those who reject Him.

People often don't like this message. It sounds too harsh. They refuse to change their lives, or they just ignore this message, as Herod did (v19–20).

TALK IT OVER

Chat with Christian friends about the idea of Jesus coming with fire and 'burning up the chaff'.

▷ *How does this make you feel?*

▷ *Do you ever mention God's judgment when talking about your faith?*

▷ *How can you talk about both forgiveness and judgment when sharing the gospel?*

PRAY ABOUT IT

Pray about these issues and the thoughts rolling around your head.

THE BOTTOM LINE

Jesus will judge everyone.

➔ TAKE IT FURTHER

A little more on the Spirit on p116.

47

Father and son

'Jesus is the Son of God.' It's easy to say, but what does it mean? And what did it mean to all those Jews around when Jesus got baptised? Step into their sandals to understand what Luke's telling us.

Read Luke 3 v 21–22

ENGAGE YOUR BRAIN

What four things are we told about Jesus in v22?

1.

2.

3.

4.

When God said: 'You are my Son', the Jews would remember those words from one of the psalms (see *Take it Further*) which says that God's King is His Son. So, God's saying that Jesus, the Son of God, is His appointed King.

When God said: *'with you I am well pleased'*, He is quoting Isaiah, where God says His servant will rescue people from sin by suffering and dying. God's saying that Jesus is His Servant who will rescue people.

John spoke and people repented and were baptised to show they'd turned from sin. Is this why Jesus was baptised? No. The Bible says He had no sin. But in the queue by the Jordan, Jesus was standing in the place of sinners.

Read verses 23–38

▷ *Why is David mentioned in the list? (Luke 1 v 32, 55, 69–70)*

Adam is also called the son of God (v38). But tomorrow, Luke will show us that Jesus is the true Son of God.

THINK IT OVER

▷ *What does it mean for us that Jesus is the Son of God?*

▷ *How does today's Bible bit show us that Jesus is unique?*

THE BOTTOM LINE

Jesus is God's Son.

→ TAKE IT FURTHER

More about Jesus on page 116.

40 Speak of the devil

Having the Holy Spirit doesn't stop Jesus from being tempted. In fact, the Spirit takes Jesus straight to a place where He can be tempted. Jesus will go three rounds with the devil. Luke is our ring-side commentator.

👁 Read Luke 4 v 1–4

ENGAGE YOUR BRAIN

▷ *How did the devil try to tempt Jesus?*

▷ *What was he hoping to achieve?*

👁 Read verses 5–8

▷ *What's wrong with the devil's offer in v6–7?*

The devil offered Jesus all the world's kingdoms. But Jesus is God's appointed King and He'll be given those anyway, as God promised in the Old Testament.

👁 Read verses 9–13

▷ *How did Jesus beat each temptation? (v4, 8, 12)*

▷ *Why do you think He dealt with the devil's attack in this way?*

If Jesus had given in to the devil, that would have been the end of God's rescue plan. Jesus kept trusting God, despite the devil's attacks. The Holy Spirit helped Him fight temptation, and He could rely on the truth of God's word from the Old Testament.

GET ON WITH IT

The more we know the Bible, the more armour we have against the devil's attacks. Spend some time now dipping into the book of *Proverbs* to find some practical advice about living for God. Pick a verse and learn it.

PRAY ABOUT IT

We must continually thank Jesus for fighting the devil's attacks and staying on His mission that led to the cross. If He hadn't, we'd have no Gospel of Luke, there'd be no Christians, and no salvation.

Also talk to God about specific temptations that don't seem to leave you alone.

➡ TAKE IT FURTHER

Tempting stuff on page 116.

41 Sweet and sour

Follow our simple recipe to create the fiery-flavoured dish Sweet and Sour Synagogue. Its first taste is sweet but it soon turns so seriously sour, it's almost a killer.

Read Luke 4 v 14–22

ENGAGE YOUR BRAIN

▷ *According to Isaiah, what five things had Jesus come to do? (v18–19)*

1.
2.
3.
4.
5.

▷ *What was the people's initial response to Jesus? (v22)*

It's a powerful scene. Jesus was in the synagogue in the town where He grew up. He read from the Old Testament and then told everyone it was about Him. Astonishing stuff.

Jesus announced His mission: preaching to the poor, bringing freedom to the oppressed, sight to the blind and to 'proclaim the year of the Lord's favour' — God rescuing His people. Jesus would release people from the devil's grasp by revealing the truth to them.

Read verses 23–30

▷ *What point was Jesus making with His history lessons? (v24–28)*

▷ *How did the crowd's mood change? (v29)*

Already, people were turning against Jesus. What Simeon told Mary was proving to be true: *'This child is destined ... to be a sign that will be spoken against.'* (Luke 2 v 34). He had come to save but not everyone wanted the sort of salvation He had come to bring. Especially if it included non-Jews.

PRAY ABOUT IT

People today just as readily reject Jesus. Many would even get rid of Him permanently if they could. Pray for people you know who fall into that category.

→ TAKE IT FURTHER

Face the opposition on page 116.

42 | Spirit splatter

So far, Luke wants his readers to know that Jesus is the Son of God and Saviour of the world, who will be accepted by some and rejected by others. It's all fulfilling what God promised in the Old Testament.

👁 Read Luke 4 v 31–34

ENGAGE YOUR BRAIN

▷ *How did people in Capernaum (v32) react differently to people in Nazareth? (v28–29)*

▷ *What did the evil spirit recognise about Jesus? (v34)*

The people of Nazareth had wanted to kill Jesus, but the Capernaum crowd were amazed at His teaching and authority. And so was the evil spirit, who recognised that Jesus was sent by God and could easily destroy evil spirits.

👁 Read verses 35–37

▷ *What did Jesus show authority over?*

▷ *What was the reaction of people in the area?*

Evil spirits could be terrifying and totally take over a person. But Jesus rules, and has power over everything. Evil spirits and murderous crowds (v30) are no match for Him. Tomorrow we'll see that illness is under His control too. Nothing is more powerful than Jesus.

THINK IT OVER

▷ *If nothing is more powerful than Jesus, how should that give us more confidence?*

▷ *What should we be afraid of?*

▷ *How can trusting Jesus' power help us as we talk to others about Him?*

PRAY ABOUT IT

Talk to God about your answers to those questions.

➡ TAKE IT FURTHER

A tiny bit more on page 117.

43 | Sickness and demons

Pack your bags and get on the tour bus. We're following Jesus on His preaching and healing tour of Judea. Yesterday we saw His authority over evil spirits. What next?

Read Luke 4 v 38–39

ENGAGE YOUR BRAIN

- What else did Jesus have power over?
- How long before Simon's mother-in-law was completely healed?

Jesus healed her instantly. In a second, she was well and back to work. Jesus has authority over illness.

Read verses 40–41

- What kinds of sickness could Jesus heal? (v40)
- Why do you think Jesus stopped the demons speaking? (v41)

Jesus had authority over every kind of illness, as well as demons and evil spirits. What power! But He wouldn't allow the demons to tell people that He was the Christ, the Son of God. It seems that Jesus wanted to show first by His words and actions what kind of Messiah He was, before He told people exactly who He was.

Read verses 42–44

- What was Jesus' job, and who sent Him to do it? (v43)

The local people wanted Jesus to stick around — He'd become very popular — but His job was to spread the good news of God's kingdom to many different kinds of people. And it was a mission from God.

Today, Luke has given us a snapshot of Jesus' life. His miracles show us that Jesus has power over **everything**. And we've seen that His priority wasn't these miracles but to teach the good news of what God was doing through His Son — so that people would follow Him and become a part of God's kingdom.

PRAY ABOUT IT

Thank Jesus for sticking to His priorities. Praise Him for having power over everything. Including us.

→ TAKE IT FURTHER

Catch up on page 117.

It's simple, Simon

Fishermen are tough lads. They have a very hard, physical job. And they smell a bit fishy too. Not really the kind of people you'd expect Jesus to hang out with.

👁 Read Luke 5 v 1–3

ENGAGE YOUR BRAIN

▷ What was Jesus doing? (v1, 3)

▷ Remember from yesterday why He was doing this?

Jesus was continuing His mission to teach God's word to people. But He wasn't just preaching from the boat...

👁 Read verses 4–11

▷ What was impressive about Simon's words? (v5)

▷ And how did he feel when he saw what Jesus had done? (v8)

▷ What surprising new job did Jesus have for these fishermen? (v10)

Jesus' command to fish some more was bizarre, as the best fishing in deep water was done at night. But there was something about Jesus that made Simon try it. When he saw the huge haul of fish, he fell to his knees and called Jesus 'Lord'. Simon also realised his own sinfulness compared to Jesus.

The nearer someone comes to God, the more they feel their own sinfulness and unworthiness to be near God. And Jesus outlined what He expects of His followers — to catch more people for Him (v10).

GET ON WITH IT

▷ When you feel close to God, do you notice your sinfulness more?

▷ How close do you feel to God right now?

▷ Anything you can do about that?

▷ How can you fish more for Jesus?

PRAY ABOUT IT

Talk over these things with God.

➡ TAKE IT FURTHER

Grab some more on page 117.

45 | Skin deep

You've probably heard about Jesus healing people with the skin disease leprosy. Pretty impressive stuff, but not worth getting excited about, right? Wrong. Having leprosy didn't just harm your skin.

👁 Read Luke 5 v 12–14

ENGAGE YOUR BRAIN

▷ What exactly did the man say Jesus could do? (v12)

▷ What did Jesus instruct him to do?

Leprosy was more than a disgusting disease. You were considered *unclean* and an outcast. You were kicked out of Jewish society, losing your family, friends, home and job. No one was allowed to come near you. It was a miserable existence.

But this man knew Jesus could make him 'clean' again, if He was willing. Imagine how the man felt as his skin tingled and was healed. Not only was he healthy again, his broken relationships could now be healed too. He was no longer an outcast. Jesus told him to go to the temple priest so his healing could be officially confirmed and he could rejoin society.

Jesus heals relationships. Especially our relationship with God. He came to ultimately die and make it possible for our broken relationship with God to be healed.

👁 Read verses 15–16

▷ What did Jesus do regularly?

Crowds of people hounded Him, wanted to hear Him and came to be healed by Him. But Jesus still found time to be on His own and pray.

PRAY ABOUT IT

We need to do the same. Do you have a time set aside each day to talk properly to God? Thank Him now for sending His Son to heal our broken relationships.

THE BOTTOM LINE

Jesus can make us clean.

➡ TAKE IT FURTHER

Prayer stuff on page 117.

46 Dropping in

Jesus had gained quite a reputation for life-changing words and astounding miracles. So much so that religious leaders flocked to see Him. And people would do anything to get their sick mates close to this healer.

👁 Read Luke 5 v 17–20

ENGAGE YOUR BRAIN

▷ What do you think the men carrying their paralysed friend hoped Jesus would do?

▷ Yet what surprising thing did He say to them? (v20)

These men were so desperate for Jesus to heal their friend that they ripped the tiles off the roof and lowered him into the house. They believed in Jesus. But the man needed to walk, so why was Jesus talking about sin?

Sin is doing what we want instead of what God wants. Sin separates us from God. This man couldn't walk, but he had a far bigger problem — **sin**.

👁 Read verses 21–26

▷ What were the Pharisees thinking? (v21)

▷ Why did Jesus heal the man? (v24)

▷ What was everyone's reaction?

The Pharisees were half-right — only God can forgive sins. But this didn't mean that Jesus was blasphemous. It meant He was God! It's much easier to say 'Your sins are forgiven' because no one can see if it's happened or not. So Jesus healed the man in front of their eyes to prove it.

THINK IT OVER

▷ Who do you think Jesus is?

▷ How would you back up your views when talking to others?

PRAY ABOUT IT

Thank God for sending Jesus to deal with our greatest problem — the need to be forgiven.

➡ TAKE IT FURTHER

Drop in to page 118 for more.

47 | Sin doctor

By His words and miraculous actions, Jesus had offended many of the religious big shots, especially the Pharisees. Imagine how they reacted to Him hanging out with 'sinners' and undesirables.

Read Luke 5 v 27–32

ENGAGE YOUR BRAIN

▷ How did Levi respond to Jesus' command to follow Him? (v28)

▷ What else did he do? (v29)

Levi was also known as Matthew — yep, the same one who wrote one of the Gospels. Tax collectors were usually dishonest and were hated. But this tax collector's life was suddenly turned upside down by Jesus. There's no other way to follow Jesus than to give up everything and follow Him completely. And Levi held a huge banquet to let everyone know. Following Jesus requires devotion and means telling others.

▷ What did the Pharisees object to? (v30)

▷ What did Jesus say His priority was?

'The righteous' means people who think they're right with God — the Pharisees, for example. They couldn't understand why Jesus would spend time with 'sinners'. But Jesus said that it was sinners — people who are aware of their sin and need for forgiveness — who He came to help. Only people like that will turn to Him to be cured of their sin disease.

PRAY ABOUT IT

Pray that your non-Christian friends will realise their sinfulness and their need to turn to Jesus for the cure. Ask God to help you tell them about Jesus, the sin doctor.

THE BOTTOM LINE

Jesus came for sinners.

→ TAKE IT FURTHER

No Take it further today, so why not spend time learning verse 32 and thinking what it means for you and people you know?

48 | Fast and furious

Pharisees thought being right with God was all about keeping laws. So Jesus explains, in three pictures, that He is bringing a real cure for sin. But it will mean a radical change.

👁 **Read Luke 5 v 33–35**

ENGAGE YOUR BRAIN

▣ *Who was the bridegroom?*

▣ *When would the disciples (wedding guests) be sad? (v35)*

The Pharisees and many other Jews fasted (went without food) twice a week as a mark of their holiness. Fasting was also a sign of sadness. But there was no reason why Jesus' disciples should fast. They were so happy to be with Jesus (the bridegroom). Why should they be sad and go without food?

Jesus knew that He would soon die. When that happened, His followers would be devastated, and then they'd fast. Yet their sorrow wouldn't last for long — God would raise Jesus back to life.

The message of Jesus was that He would die to rescue people from sin. But the Pharisees said you had to keep a set of rules to be right with God. The two messages don't mix.

👁 **Read verses 36-39**

▣ *Why doesn't Jesus' new message mix with the Pharisees' old one? (v37)*

Trying to fit the message of Jesus into a human set of rules won't work. The Pharisees said: *'You must keep our rules to please God'*. Jesus said: *'Repent (turn away from your sin) and believe the good news'*.

You can't become a Christian by keeping rules or being good. Only by **trusting Jesus** to forgive your sin.

PRAY ABOUT IT

Thank God that you don't need to keep a set of rules to be made right with Him. Thank Him for sending Jesus as Saviour. Ask Him to help you share the message of Jesus.

➔ **TAKE IT FURTHER**

More fast facts on page 117.

TOOLBOX

So what?

One of the main ambitions of **engage** is to encourage you to get stuck into God's word. Each issue, TOOLBOX gives you tips, tools and advice for wrestling with the Bible and understanding it more.

It's possible to read the Bible, and even to understand it well, without it having any effect on you at all. Unless we recognise that God is actually speaking to us through His word, it's a waste of time. When we read the Bible we should always ask 'So what?'

DO WHAT IT SAYS

We need to make sure we understand what we're reading before we apply the teaching. But we must also be careful to actually learn from and do whatever God is teaching us.

'Do not merely listen to the word, and so deceive yourselves. Do what it says.' (James 1 v 22)

So how can we make sure that we actually do what the Bible says? Stage 1 is to work out what response the author was looking for. Stage 2 is to make that happen in the nitty-gritty of our lives. Here are two questions that might help:

▷ *Is there something I should stop doing? Is there some aspect of my behaviour that must change?*

▷ *Is there something new that I need to start doing?*

MOTIVES MATTER

Simply doing an action isn't enough on its own. The motive that lies behind it is important too. Sometimes we're given direct commands:

'Flee from sexual immorality.' (1 Corinthians 6 v 18)

Obviously, the right response to a verse like this is to put it into practice and obey what God says. However, our motives matter too. We can sometimes do things to impress other Christians, or because we think doing good deeds makes us right with God. We need to do stuff for the right reasons.

'Flee from sexual immorality. All other sins a man commits are outside his body, but he who sins sexually sins against his own body. Do you not know that your body is a temple of the Holy Spirit, who is in you, whom you have received from God? You are not your own; you were bought at a price. Therefore honour God with your body.' (1 Corinthians 6 v 18–20)

Paul gives us motivation for fleeing sexual immorality:

- *We have the Holy Spirit living in us, so what we do with our bodies really matters.*
- *We've been bought by God so we now belong to Him.*

Not only does the Bible show us how to live God's way, it tells us why we should live differently.

WHO'S IT FOR?

Not every passage of the Bible will be equally relevant at every point in your life. Some passages are written to comfort people who are suffering; others to warn against specific sin — they are for different times in your life. However, don't be too selective in what you read; the ideal is to work through whole books bit by bit, and to cover the whole Bible eventually. This way you'll store up lessons that you might need in the future when circumstances change. And it stops you from steering clear of uncomfortable passages which — like bad-tasting medicine — are still really good for you.

Sometimes you'll hear God saying something in the Bible that you realise would be a great help to somebody else. Sharing God's truth with another Christian can be a hugely encouraging thing. At other times, the Bible's message will apply to the whole church (see Hebrews 3 v 12). We also need to look out for when a particular Bible bit has implications for our non-Christian friends (see John 3 v 35–36).

You need to ask what a Bible passage means...
- *for you*
- *for a Christian friend*
- *for your church/youth group*
- *for non-Christians you know*

Merely reading God's word isn't enough — we've got to act on it. When you read a Bible passage, think:

1. So what?
2. Who is this Bible passage for?
3. What do I need to do about what I've read?
4. What's the reason behind doing this?

Ideas taken from Dig Deeper by Nigel Beynon and Andrew Sach (available from Good Book Company website).

Exodus: Payback time

Back to Exodus and God's ground rules for His people. This next section deals with the Israelites' possessions and property — think back to God's commands not to steal or covet/lust after other people's things.

Read Exodus 22 v 1–17

ENGAGE YOUR BRAIN

▷ Have a quick look at each of the examples given in v1-15. What is the offender to do every time?

▷ How does compensating someone affect both the owner and the thief?

▷ Do you think this is a good principle for dealing with these kinds of issues?

One of the big ideas in this section is trust and justice. The Israelites needed to be able to trust their neighbours and be sure they wouldn't lose out because of someone else's actions. So v16 isn't talking about rape, but someone trying to get the benefits of marrying a virgin without giving the expected 'payment' to compensate her father for losing a daughter.

▷ Do people know that you won't take advantage of them or use them for your own benefit?

As Christians, our standards should reflect God's. *'He who has been stealing must steal no longer, but must work, doing something useful with his own hands, that he may have something to share with those in need'* (Ephesians 4 v 28).

PRAY ABOUT IT

What should be Christians' attitudes to other people and their possessions? Is there anything you need to repent of? Talk to God.

GET ON WITH IT

You might not have robbed any banks recently, but is there anything you need to make amends for? Wasting time that you were trusted to use for study or work? Taking advantage of someone's good nature to get away with behaviour that isn't up to God's standards?

→ TAKE IT FURTHER

Steal away to page 118.

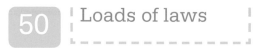

50 Loads of laws

More laws now. These might seem like a random mixture to begin with. But look at what they tell us about God.

Read Exodus 22 v 18 – 23 v 9

ENGAGE YOUR BRAIN

Fill in the table below.

Verse	What is banned?	Why? What does it tell us about God?
22v18	Sorcery	Puts trust in power other than God.
19	Bestiality	Disgusting! God's expects purity.
20		
21-27		
28		
29-30		
31		
23v1-3		
4-5		
6-7		
8		
9		

PRAY ABOUT IT

Look at everything you've learned about God.
Spend some time now thanking and praising Him for who He is.

TAKE IT FURTHER

More on page 118.

51 Festival season

What do you enjoy most about Christmas? What about Easter? Just like the Israelite festivals, these things weren't designed simply for our enjoyment. They remind us of something much deeper.

👁 Read Exodus 23 v 10–13

ENGAGE YOUR BRAIN

▷ *What is the pattern for work on a big scale (years) and small a scale (every week)?*

▷ *Which commandment does this remind us of? (clue: 20 v 8)*

Months and years are defined by natural phenomena such as the phases of the moon or the earth's journey round the sun. But there is no reason in nature why our weeks are 7 days long. This pattern of 6 days on, one day off or even six years farming, one year of rest, makes brilliant sense practically. It avoids burnout or over-farming — but also points us to our Creator. God created the universe in 6 days and then rested.

▷ *How does God again spell out what matters to Him most? (v13)*

👁 Read verses 14–19

▷ *What are the three annual festivals each to remind the Israelites of?*

Christians don't have the same festivals as the Jews of Moses' day, but we do have points in the year which help to remember important things about God.

▷ *What does Christmas remind you of?*

▷ *And Easter?*

PRAY ABOUT IT

Spend some time thanking God for sending Jesus to earth, to die for our sins. Thank Him that He rose to new life and is now in heaven.

THE BOTTOM LINE

God is at the centre of every year and every week.

→ TAKE IT FURTHER

Check out page 118.

52 | Guardian angel

Some more amazing promises now as God lays out His plans for bringing the Israelites to their new home.

👁 **Read Exodus 23 v 20–33**

ENGAGE YOUR BRAIN

▷ *What incredible things was God going to do for His people? List them below:*

▷ *What would they have to do?*

▷ *What does God warn them against once more? (v32-33)*

Look at that great list of promises God gives the Israelites. He is so good and generous to them and all they have to do is trust and obey Him. But will they? The rest of the Old Testament tells the sorry story of how they failed time after time to do that.

It becomes clear that a new kind of 'exodus' will be needed, a new escape from 'slavery', a new Moses. And God's people will need new hearts — hearts that want to trust and obey God and a new spirit that will enable them to do it.

👁 **Read Jeremiah 31 v 31–34**

👁 **Read Ezekiel 11 v 19–20**

PRAY ABOUT IT

Those verses are fulfilled in Jesus. He is the one who rescues us from slavery to sin and who gives us His Holy Spirit so that we can live for God. Spend some time thanking Him right now.

THE BOTTOM LINE

God is faithful to His promises even when His people are not.

→ **TAKE IT FURTHER**

Grab some more on page 118.

53 | Holy smoke

Having heard God's laws, we now get a glimpse of the people's reaction to them. It looks good so far....

Read Exodus 24 v 1–18

ENGAGE YOUR BRAIN

▷ *Who can get close to God? (v1-2)*

Again we see how holy God is — not just anyone can walk up to Him. But He still makes a covenant (an agreement, a formal relationship) with the Israelites (v8).

▷ *What did the people promise to do — twice?*

The Israelites' obedience was a response to being rescued. The same is true for Christians — look at Jesus' words before He returned to heaven: *'All authority in heaven and on earth has been given to me. Therefore go and make disciples of all nations, baptising them in the name of the Father and of the Son and of the Holy Spirit, **and teaching them to obey everything I have commanded you**. And surely I am with you always, to the very end of the age.'* (Matthew 28 v 18–20)

GET ON WITH IT

▷ *Are you obeying Jesus?*

▷ *How can you obey this command more?*

ENGAGE YOUR BRAIN

▷ *What did God say He was going to give Moses? (v12)*

▷ *What shows us just how close to God Moses was? (v15–18)*

We're reminded over and over in this section of Exodus just how incredibly powerful and holy God is. Do you really grasp that? Do you appreciate how wonderful it is that you can have a relationship with Him because of Jesus? Spend some time thanking Him now.

→ TAKE IT FURTHER
Grab more on page 119.

54 | Live-in Lord

Having just seen how difficult it is for sinful people to get close to a holy God, Moses receives a mind-blowing piece of information...

👁 Read Exodus 25 v 1–9

ENGAGE YOUR BRAIN

▶ *How does God describe the way these offerings will be given? (v2)*

▶ *What was the amazing news for God's people? (v8)*

▶ *What will that mean for Israel?*

God has always wanted to live with His people. Think back to Adam and Eve in the garden — God walked and talked with them until they rebelled against Him. Now He is promising Israel that He will live among them.

▶ *What are the benefits of that promise?*

▶ *What are the dangers?*

The tabernacle (literally a big tent) was the first stage in God's plan to live with His people. Later, the temple would be the place where God met with them and, still later, the ultimate way in which God would live with humanity would be in Jesus. One of Jesus' other names is *'Emmanuel'*, which means *'God with us'*.

PRAY ABOUT IT

Thank God that He is not distant and uncaring but wants to know us and be with us.

THE BOTTOM LIFE

God wants to live with His people. How mind-blowing is that?

➡ TAKE IT FURTHER

Living proof on page 119.

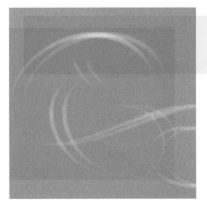

55 | The mercy seat

Most of the instructions to do with the tabernacle (where God was present among the Israelites) and what went inside it point out two facts: 1) God is holy and 2) People are sinful.

Read Exodus 25 v 10–16

ENGAGE YOUR BRAIN

▶ What do you think all the gold shows us?

▶ What is to go inside the ark?

At the centre of God's tabernacle is the Testimony — two stone tablets with the Ten Commandments inscribed on them. The most important thing for God's people must be His covenant, His commands.

If you want to know about God (what He's like), you can read about Him in the Bible. But you also need to get to know Jesus, who is the only way to know God personally.

GET ON WITH IT

So what can you do to get the Bible into more people's hands? Maybe you could give friends a Bible or gospel and chat about it with them. Or you could raise money for Bible translators like Wycliffe. (www.wycliffe.org.uk)

Read verses 17–22

▶ How is the cover of the ark described? (v17)

The mercy seat was where blood from sacrifices of atonement was sprinkled, so that the people's sins could be forgiven.

▶ Again, what are we reminded about the ark's contents? (v21)

▶ Why do you think God's perfect law needed to be 'covered' with a place for sacrifice?

▶ What is the amazing promise of v22?

PRAY ABOUT IT

Thank God that although we break His law, He provides a way for our sins to be forgiven so that He can be with us. Thank Him that Jesus paid for sins once and for all with His blood, on the cross.

➡ TAKE IT FURTHER

Be law-abiding on page 119.

56 | Table manners

Have you ever seen anyone offering food to their gods? It always seems a bit odd, rather like leaving a mince pie out for Santa. So what is going on in these next verses?

👁 Read Exodus 25 v 23–30

ENGAGE YOUR BRAIN

▶ *What materials is this table made of?*

▶ *What does that tell you about it?*

▶ *What will go on the table?*

The bread of the presence was for the priests to eat — Israelites who were set apart to serve God in the tabernacle. So the bread was a way of showing how God fed them and provided for them. It wasn't food for God.

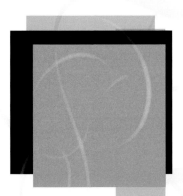

Acts 17 v 25 tells us that God *"is not served by human hands, as if he needed anything, because he himself gives all men life and breath and everything else."*

Do you ever fall into the trap of thinking that you are doing stuff for God? That He should be really pleased with what you are doing for Him? A wise friend once said to me: 'God has more to do in you than through you'.

PRAY ABOUT IT

Spend some time asking God to help you see things from His perspective.

THE BOTTOM LINE

God provides for His people.

➡ TAKE IT FURTHER

Eat more bread on page 119.

57 | See the light

Why is light important?
What would life be like, living in the dark?

👁 Read Exodus 25 v 31–40

ENGAGE YOUR BRAIN

▷ *What is the lampstand to be made of?*

▷ *What does it look like?*

Gold, light and flame are all things associated with God in the Bible, so this impressive lampstand is therefore a good reminder of God's presence with His people. Some people think the tree-like shape of the lampstand was supposed to be like the burning bush, but whatever the significance, it is yet another indication of God's holiness.

It was one of the priest's key duties to keep the lamp burning at all times, so it was obviously important (see Exodus 27 v 20–21).

👁 Read Revelation 21 v 22–24

▷ *How will the new creation be even better than the tabernacle?*

▷ *Who is the Lamb?*

▷ *How is He like a lamp to people?*

One day, all God's people will go to live with Him for ever. There will be no need for the sun or moon because God's glory will provide enough light. There will be no more darkness. We'll live in the light of God's glory and perfection. Jesus — the Lamb of God — is like a lamp showing people the way to go.

PRAY ABOUT IT

Ask God to help you live in the light — following His Son. Thank Him that one day His people will live with Him in perfection.

THE BOTTOM LINE

God is light. In Him there is no darkness at all.

➡ TAKE IT FURTHER

Lighten up on page 119.

58 | In tents

Bored of the tabernacle and all the descriptions of furniture. Well, it may sound unimportant, but it all points us to some vital truths about God.

Read Exodus 26 v 1–37

ENGAGE YOUR BRAIN

▶ *What are the curtains like? (v1, v31, v36)*

▶ *What other materials are used?*

The colours and fabrics used make the tabernacle seem more like a king's royal pavilion — not a tent. Again we see precious metals, lots of gold in particular, highlighting God's kingly and holy credentials.

The tabernacle, once constructed, would have looked a bit like this:

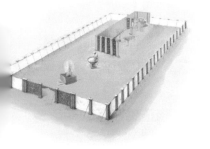

▶ *What was inside the central Most Holy Place? (v33–34)*

▶ *What was outside the holy place? (v35)*

God was with His people, but no ordinary person could approach Him in the Most Holy Place. Not until...

PRAY ABOUT IT

When Jesus died, the curtain in the temple (a permanent version of the tabernacle) was torn in two, from top to bottom. Jesus' death means that anyone can now have access to God. That would have blown Moses' mind. Thank God for His incredible goodness in sending Jesus to open the way.

THE BOTTOM LINE

Through Jesus we have access to our holy God.

➔ TAKE IT FURTHER

More on how to get to God on page 120.

59 | At the altar

We're moving out of the tabernacle and into the courtyard — where blood would be shed...

👁 Read Exodus 27 v 1–21

ENGAGE YOUR BRAIN

▷ What is to be used most in decorating the courtyard?

▷ What do you think happened in the courtyard? (v1–3)

▷ What fact about the people's relationship with God does this highlight?

Notice the 'sprinkling bowls' in v3. For sins to be forgiven, for an unclean people to approach a pure and holy God, sacrifice needed to be made, blood needed to be shed.

An animal (cow, sheep or goat) would be brought to the altar (which was roughly the size of a small bedroom), and slaughtered by the priest. Then it would be burned on the altar as an offering to God.

TALK IT OVER

Hebrews 10 v 3–4 tells us: *'Those sacrifices are an annual reminder of sins, because it is impossible for the blood of bulls and goats to take away sins'*. Chat with another Christian about why this system couldn't fully sort out the problem of human sin.

Jesus' perfect life is now the only sacrifice God will accept for our sin.

PRAY ABOUT IT

At the last supper Jesus said to his disciples: *'This is my blood of the covenant, which is poured out for many for the forgiveness of sins'* (Matthew 26 v 28).

▷ Have you accepted that Jesus' blood is the only way you can be forgiven?

THE BOTTOM LINE

Sin is fatal. Thank God for Jesus.

➡ TAKE IT FURTHER

More sin stuff on page 120.

60 Priests on the catwalk

The focus now shifts from the tabernacle to the priests — the men chosen by God to represent His people. First we get a quick fashion show...

👁 Read Exodus 28 v 1–14

ENGAGE YOUR BRAIN

▷ *What do you notice about the garments (v5)? How are they similar to the materials of the tabernacle?*

▷ *What point does v12 make about Aaron's role?*

👁 Read Exodus 28 v 29–38

▷ *What does v35 remind us about God?*

▷ *What do we learn about the priests? (v36-38)*

Next we learn in chapter 29 about how the priests and the tabernacle are to be 'consecrated' — set apart and devoted to the service of God.

👁 Read Exodus 29 v 42–46

▷ *What is the point of all of the sacrifice and ritual? (v46)*

The detail of this may seem very alien to us, but is that because we have got too used to the free access we have to our God? God is still terrifyingly holy. Human beings are still unbelievably sinful. When we read these Old Testament descriptions of how difficult it was for Israel to get close to their God, we should be amazed and thankful for Jesus bringing us so close to God.

PRAY ABOUT IT

'With a loud cry, Jesus breathed his last. The curtain of the temple was torn in two from top to bottom' (Mark 15 v 37–38). Spend some time thinking, thanking and praising God.

→ TAKE IT FURTHER

For the rest of these two chapters, turn to page 120.

STUFF

Alcohol and drugs

Al likes the occasional drink but never gets drunk. Well, maybe at parties. Col is going to uni soon and wonders whether he'll try marijuana just to see what the buzz is about. Holly thinks all drugs and alcohol are evil and criticises any Christian who even sets foot in a pub.

Do any of these characters seem familiar to you?

WHAT'S THE BIG DEAL?

Well, the Bible doesn't say much specifically about recreational drugs, but it has plenty to say about alcohol, addiction, temptation and looking after yourself. Obviously, it's illegal to buy alcohol below a certain age and God wants us to keep the law (Romans 13 v 1), but alcohol itself isn't evil. Jesus' first miracle was to turn water into fine wine at a wedding feast (John 2 v 1–11). Psalm 104 tells us that God created *'wine that gladdens the heart of man'*. Paul even encouraged Timothy to drink a little wine when he was ill (1 Timothy 5 v 23).

As with anything, the problem with alcohol is when we consume too much. The book of Proverbs points out the mess we can get into when we drink too much. *'Wine is a mocker and beer a brawler; whoever is led astray by them is not wise'* (Proverbs 20 v 1).

SNAKE POISON

It's easy to fall into regular drinking habits and even drunkenness without noticing it happen: *'Do not gaze at wine when it is red, when it sparkles in the cup, when it goes down smoothly! In the end it bites like a snake and poisons like a viper. Your eyes will see strange sights and your mind imagine confusing things. You will be like one sleeping on the high seas, lying on top of the rigging. "They hit me," you will say, "but I'm not hurt! They beat me, but I don't feel it! When will I wake up so I can find another drink?"* (Proverbs 23 v 31–35). Alcohol is addictive and it can grab hold of you.

But your drinking can cause problems for others too, not just yourself. Younger Christians may see you as a role model, so make sure you act in a way that honours God. Some Christians are very anti-alcohol (often for good reasons). Romans chapter 14 is all about issues like this that divide believers. Paul says that arguing over things like this shouldn't get in the way of God's work. If your drinking is a big problem to people around you, why not give it up for a while? And if you have doubts about whether or not something is right or wrong, DON'T DO IT! (Romans 14 v 23) That way you can be sure you're not disobeying God.

WHAT ABOUT DRUGS?

It's a no-brainer that drugs are out of the picture for Christians — using them is illegal and the evidence of how harmful they are can be seen in the faces and lives of any addict. And yet it can still be so tempting to try it. James says: *'Resist the devil and*

he will flee from you' (James 4 v 7). Fight tempting urges. In fact, God has promised to always give us a way out of every temptation (1 Corinthians 10 v 13), so make sure you grab it.

Treat your body as a temple, devoted to God (1 Corinthians 6 v 19–20). And if you find yourself falling for alcohol, drugs or any other sinful temptation, grab some Christian mates and ask them to help you and pray for you (James 5 v 16). It may be difficult and embarrassing, but it really does work. God wants to help you out of any tight spot so you can get back to living His way.

Ultimately, we don't need to look elsewhere for highs — God gives us everything we need. Nothing can beat the high of God's Spirit working in us, making us more like Jesus. *'Do not get drunk on wine, which leads to debauchery. Instead, be filled with the Spirit'* (Ephesians 5 v 18).

61 | PSALMS: Shameless

Life is sometimes lonely and difficult. We can feel out of control or lost. David — who wrote this psalm — knows how it feels.

Read Psalm 25

ENGAGE YOUR BRAIN

- When does David come to God? (v5 and 15)
- What does he share with God? (v1 and 16-21)
- Which verses show David was a sinner?

Think you have to be perfect to pray for God's help? David was far from perfect yet he still had the confidence to ask God for some big things. David's demands and needs are big, but God is bigger.

In v19 David mentions his enemies. Our greatest enemy is Satan — he hates us (v19) and tries to trap us in sin and guilt (ensnares us – v15). He relishes the fact we've all done things to be ashamed of.

On spare paper, write down stuff you've done which you know is wrong — 'fessing up is the first part of your strategy to thrash Satan.

Then, get the fattest pen you can find. Write v20 across your confessions in large letters!

- What does David ask God to remember? (v6-7)
- And to forget?
- According to this psalm, what is God like?

Interestingly, David doesn't ask God to remember what a good guy he's been (he knows he hasn't). He asks God to remember what a merciful, loving God He is. Awesome news! God's rescue plan is trustworthy because it depends on His perfection, not ours.

PRAY ABOUT IT

Read v1–7 out loud to God as a prayer (unless you're on the bus, in which case, read it in your head), praying it to God.

➡ TAKE IT FURTHER

Fight the devil on page 120.

62 Clear-cut Christian

You meet another Christian at a party. Can they tell from your behaviour that you're a Christian too? Maybe it's not always obvious — but don't give up! God's great at taking our tarnished lives and creating clear-cut Christians.

👁 **Read Psalm 26**

ENGAGE YOUR BRAIN

▷ What does David want God to do? (v1–3)
▷ Why?

David knew he was sinful, but he also knew he needed to live God's way. David's saying: 'Prove I'm right to live your way, Lord.' Can you relate to that prayer? Been dissed for not getting drunk? Seen as a bit sad for respecting God's laws on sex and relationships?

Obeying God is totally worth it. Living blamelessly ultimately leads to eternal life. But isn't David an ordinary sinner? Why's he now harping on about his 'blameless life'?

▷ What's a blameless life? Write a summary of each verse with your own words:
eg: v1 Always trust in God.
v2:
v3:
v4–6:
v7:
v8:

Are v4-5 saying: 'Non-Christian friends are not allowed'? Nope. We should share God's greatness with them (v7). But we shouldn't share their lifestyle. David avoids 'evildoers' to avoid temptation, knowing he's not good enough to survive in their company.

TALK IT OVER
Do any of your friends drag you away from God? Chat to an older Christian about it.

PRAY ABOUT IT
If you love Jesus, God sees you as blameless. You've been forgiven. Look back at the hallmarks of a blameless life. Pick one you need to work at. Ask for God's help.

➔ **TAKE IT FURTHER**
Battle with sin on page 121.

63 | Cross-eyed

Ever been in an exam where it's all going wrong? Ever tried talking to yourself to calm yourself down? (It's the first sign of madness apparently; the second is standing in your garden with custard-filled pants.)

Read Psalm 27

ENGAGE YOUR BRAIN

This psalm is like eavesdropping on David as he tries to calm down by shouting out great truths about God. Find them and list them below:

God is magnificent. Yet He is not distant. He can be found. He uses His power to save, shelter and protect those who seek Him.

GET ON WITH IT

Don't panic! Remember God. Learn v1 now — it's a great stress-buster.

Check out v3. Facing military action? Probably not. Change the words to fit your life at the moment eg: *'Though*

arguments with family besiege me…'

Now, personalise v4: *'One thing I ask of the LORD…'*

How did your one request compare to David's? God-centred like his, or self-centred? Despite the carnage surrounding him, David's looking towards God and eternity.

▷ *Is God reliable during troubles? (v5)*
▷ *Is He a good God? (v13)*

PRAY ABOUT IT

God is always reliable, but don't take Him for granted. God would be fully justified in turning us away because of His anger at our sin (v9). We need to be like David, begging for mercy (v7). We need to remember the cross, where God's mercy is poured out through Jesus. Do that now.

→ TAKE IT FURTHER

Tell yourself you need to check out *Take it further* on page 121.

64 The shield

What gives you the confidence to come to our all-powerful God in prayer? If you're not sure, Psalm 28 should give your prayers a confidence-boost.

Read Psalm 28 v1–2

ENGAGE YOUR BRAIN

What does David ask for?

If God stays silent, what would David be like?

David can cry out to the Lord because He's approachable. David is lost without God guiding him.

Read verses 3–5

What's David's shockingly honest request in v4?

If we ignore God's works, what will happen?

David's very blunt! When reading stuff like this, always remember that David's job description, as king, also made him a judge.

God will justly punish evil. However, punishment is escapable. Not through 'being good', but by respecting God's works. God's ultimate work was Jesus' death in the place of sinners.

Read verses 6–7

How do v6–7 give hope and comfort?

Realising God is a fair Judge can be terrifying. The only shield we have against God's judgment is…Him (v7). He hears our cry for mercy, offering protection through Jesus' death. Does that make your heart leap for joy? (It should!) Thank God now.

Read verses 8–9

How is God described here?

David's final focus is on God's strength and compassion, leaving no doubt God will protect His people for ever.

PRAY ABOUT IT

God is approachable and He hears. Make the most of it! Pray about areas where you need help.

→ TAKE IT FURTHER

More stuff on page 121.

65 | Stormin' stuff

How do you picture God? A grandfather figure in white robes and a beard, floating on a cloud? An invisible force? Something else? Let's read Psalm 29 for a reality check.

Read Psalm 29 v1–9

ENGAGE YOUR BRAIN

▷ Why should God be given glory? (v2)

▷ How would you describe God after reading these verses?

▷ What's the only right response to this awesome God? (end of v9)

David seems to have written this psalm in the middle of a huge and terrifying storm that reminded him of how powerful and terrifying God can be.

Ascribe means 'give credit where credit's due'. And the mighty ones (v1) are probably angels. These verses point to how incredibly powerful and fearsome God is. He deserves glory and worship for who He is. We should give it to Him.

Read verses 10–11

▷ How great is God? (v10)

▷ People often ask 'Where is God?' What's the answer? (v10)

▷ How gracious is God? (v11)

God is so glorious, David's human praise is inadequate; he must call on angels to help worship this God who shakes the earth simply by the power of His voice.

PRAY ABOUT IT

Spend time praising our awesome, fearsome, yet gracious God. And pray v11 for Christians in the world's disaster zones.

→ TAKE IT FURTHER

Thunder along to page 121.

66 | Rollercoaster psalm

Is your life a bit of a rollercoaster? David probably never went to his local Jerusalem theme park for a ride on the 'Deadly Corkscrew', but his psalms brilliantly reflect life's highs and lows. Psalm 30 is a great example.

👁 Read Psalm 30 v 1–3

ENGAGE YOUR BRAIN

▷ What did David do when he was in 'the depths'? (v2)

▷ How did God respond?

▷ Do you pray for healing when you're ill?

👁 Read verses 4–7

A 'saint' isn't some totally perfect, golden boy, halo gleaming in the secure knowledge he's never, ever sinned. When the Bible talks about saints, it simply means people who trust in Jesus. Christians.

▷ Saints still mess up and sin, provoking God's anger. What's the good news for them in v5?

▷ What is David's response to God's care? (v6)

'Rejoicing in the morning' (v5). The ultimate 'morning' for Christians is eternal life. Even if life on earth is full of weeping, we always have the rejoicing-filled hope of eternal life with God.

👁 Read verses 8–12

▷ Which characteristics of God give hope in despair?

▷ What's happened to David's wailing and mourning?

Interestingly, God's ultimate purpose in transforming David's grief is to bring glory to Himself.

PRAY ABOUT IT

Think of a seemingly hopeless situation you are going through. Pray about it to God – the great Hope-giver, who has transforming power.

⇒ TAKE IT FURTHER

Enjoy the ride on page 121.

REAL LIVES

Why me?

Each month in REAL LIVES, we bring you stories of people whose lives have been transformed by Christ. This issue, we talk to someone who as a teenager discovered they had a serious illness. Article by Fiona Simmons.

When did you find out you had Crohn's disease?

I was fourteen when the doctor diagnosed me. Crohn's is an inflammatory disease caused by an overactive immune system. The hardest thing at the time was stopping myself asking: *'Why me?'* There I was, living as a Christian, and a relatively good person, and I was sick. Why was the horrible person down the road fit and healthy? That was hard to get to grips with, because try as you might, you do want to get better.

And as you began to come to terms with having a chronic illness, what was the hardest thing?

I think it was other people not understanding what I could and couldn't do. I was hugely tired and people still expected me to

> God gives pain for a reason — it's to make you more like Jesus.

do everything they were doing. In parties, people would offer me food that I wasn't allowed in my exclusion diet. When I came in to school late after being in hospital, the attendance officer would tell me off. Of course, none of them knew, or realised how hard it was, but that didn't stop it being hugely difficult. I had been taught that I'd never be alone, and that God was always with me. And that's easy to tell other people, but less easy to believe.

Did you pray for healing?

Don't you start! One of the strangest parts of being ill in church was people telling me that it was all about faith — if I had faith and prayed hard for healing, then God would heal me. But really, I knew that might not happen. In fact, later on, I turned it round: I started asking myself, *'Why do I deserve healing and someone else doesn't?'* I think it made me grow up quite a lot.

Were there any good things to come out of your illness?

It definitely made me a more mature Christian. I remember having a chat with my mum, having to realise that I was ill, but that I still trusted God. He can choose who He heals. I can't twist God's arm. It's a lot for a fourteen-year-old; it makes you ask: *'Is God good?'* But it's not that terrible — there are worse things, like hell, for example! A lot of people said it was awful that such a young person was so ill. That it was unfair, somehow. But it's not the most important thing to be healthy. It made me face my mortality, which young people don't have to think about much.

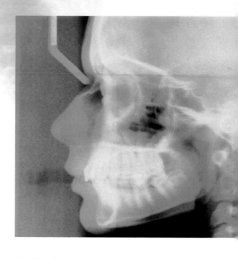

What particular things did your illness teach you?

It taught me things like God gives you pain for a reason — it's to make you more like Jesus. Although you don't know exactly what's going on, remember it's a fallen world. Your suffering isn't a result of your personal sin. The disciples saw a blind man and asked Jesus: *'Who has sinned, this man or his parents?'* and the answer was neither (John 9 v 1–3).

What would you say to other Christians suffering with illness?

I would say don't assume you'll be healed. You might be, but don't take that as given. Also, don't waste your illness — use the opportunities it gives you to talk about Jesus. It did actually make me able to talk to people who are ill or depressed and sympathise with them, which I couldn't do before. To know a bit better how to care for them — it humbled me. It made me think about helping people with illness, and so I'm much better than I was in that respect.

Do you think you might get better?

Crohn's is treatable, if not curable, so I'm on medication to keep it at bay, having had a major operation at eighteen. But Crohn's always comes back, and after having it for years now, I am beginning to understand. Hospital feels like home and I can't do everything I want to do, but that doesn't matter. I think it's much more profitable to put my hope in heaven. It's a much stronger anchor.

67 Romans: Sin disease

We're turning back to Paul's letter to Christians in Rome. So far, he's pointed out that no one is good enough to meet God's perfect standards — but while we were still sinners, Christ died for us.

👁 Read Romans 5 v 12–14

ENGAGE YOUR BRAIN

▷ Who have sinned and deserve to be punished with death? (v12)

▷ Who sinned first?

▷ So why is it that we all deserve to be punished?

Adam disobeyed God, bringing sin into the world. God's punishment was death — Adam died. And death has also been the end for every human since. Sin is like a disease. Adam brought it into the world and spread it around. Sin entered the world through Adam and Eve, but we've all caught the sin disease by disobeying God. We're all just as bad.

When Adam fell into sin, we all fell with him. But there's no point blaming him and thinking we could have done any better. Every one of us has chosen to sin. Chosen to live for ourselves instead of living for God.

Adam, the first man, sinned for all of us. But we've all sinned too. Adam brought death into the world. But we all deserve death because we're all sinners. Tomorrow, Paul will tell us all about the cure, which he hints at in v14.

PRAY ABOUT IT

We're all naturally sinful. Ask God to help you fight specific sins that hound you. And pray for friends who don't yet realise they need a cure for their sin disease.

THE BOTTOM LINE

By one man's sin, everyone was plunged into sin, guilt and death.

→ TAKE IT FURTHER

More sin stuff on page 122.

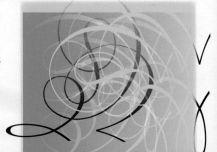

68 | Full of life

Yesterday Paul told us the tragic truth — one man (Adam) plunged us all into sin and death. Today he gives us the good news — one Man (Jesus) can rescue us from sin and death.

👁 Read Romans 5 v 15–17

ENGAGE YOUR BRAIN

▷ *How much more did Jesus do than Adam? (v15–16)*

▷ *What's the result for those who receive God's great gift? (v17)*

Jesus did far more than reverse the death sentence brought by Adam's sin. Out of His overflowing grace pour the riches of eternal life! Freedom from sin and the gift of eternal life are on offer for all who receive them, by trusting in Jesus. Earth–shattering stuff.

👁 Read verses 18–21

▷ *What was the result of Adam's action? (v18)*

▷ *And what about Jesus' action? (v18–19)*

▷ *What's Paul's point in v20–21?*

Adam may have brought sin and God's punishment into the world, but Jesus Christ has made it possible for us to be made right with God and experience eternal life, through *'one act of righteousness'* — His death on the cross.

Verses 20–21 are slightly tricky. They say that God's law in the Old Testament shows up our sin — it shows us that we fail to obey God. Once we realise how sinful we are, we're more likely to ask for God's forgiveness. That's God's grace at work, bringing people to eternal life through Jesus.

PRAY ABOUT IT

If you're a Christian and you're not bursting with excitement and thanks to God right now, there's something seriously wrong.

➡ TAKE IT FURTHER

More on page 122.

69 | Evil twin

A pair of twins look the same, sound the same, but aren't the same age. They were born years apart. The first one died at exactly the time the second was born. How can this be? Well, they're both you if you're a Christian.

👁 Read Romans 6 v 1–4

ENGAGE YOUR BRAIN

▷ If Christians' sins are forgiven, can they carry on sinning? (v1–2)

Jesus died on the cross to take the punishment we deserve. He died for our sin. So when you become a Christian you have all your wrongs forgiven by Jesus. It is as though your sinful life has died with Jesus. You no longer want to disobey God; you want to please Him. That's the plan, anyway.

Back in Jesus' time, everyone who chose to follow Him was baptised — it symbolised the death of their old, sinful life. Twin one was dead: twin two was now alive, living for Jesus. People who trust in Jesus have *shared* in Jesus' death and *shared* in Jesus' resurrection. Stop and take that in for a moment.

👁 Read verses 5–7

▷ What has happened to our old, sinful twin? (v6)

▷ So what's true of our new life as a Christian? (v7)

Our old self dies when we trust in Jesus and His death in our place. We're born again, freed from the grip sin had on our lives. Free to serve God. Yes, we'll still mess up sometimes, but sin no longer rules us — God does.

PRAY ABOUT IT

Thank God that He frees His people from sin. Ask Him to help you with specific temptations you battle with.

THE BOTTOM LINE

A Christian's sinful self has died.

→ TAKE IT FURTHER

More about baptism on page 122.

70 Alive and kicking

Christians are dead to sin — it no longer rules them. So why do we still struggle to say 'no' to sin and temptation? How do we make sure our sin is put to death?

👁 Read Romans 6 v 8–11

ENGAGE YOUR BRAIN

▷ *Who did Jesus live for? (v10)*

▷ *So who do Christians (Christ-followers) live for?*

Christians share in Jesus' death and also in His risen life. They are dead to sin — it no longer rules them. It's as if they have become fully alive to God for the first time. Verse 10 calls this living to God instead of living to sin.

THINK IT OVER

▷ *In your attitude, have you drawn a line under sin or have you left the door open to it coming back?*

▷ *Yes, we still fail — but what can you do to kick sin from your life?*

▷ *How can you be more committed to living for God?*

👁 Read verses 12–14

▷ *What does Paul tell Christians not to do? (v12–13)*

▷ *So what should Christians do?*

▷ *Think of specific things you need to stop doing, and start doing.*

It's going to be hard, so don't miss the great promise in v14. If you're a Christian you're dead to sin and alive in Christ. So live like it — get pleasing God and kick out the wrong stuff in your life. Don't think about going back to sinful living. How could you when you've shared in Jesus' death and resurrection?

PRAY ABOUT IT

Read through v13 and pray about the issues it raises.

THE BOTTOM LINE

Christians are dead to sin and alive to God.

→ TAKE IT FURTHER

More sin-battling on page 122.

85

71 | Slaving away

How do you feel about being a slave? It's not a positive thought, is it? Paul says we're all slaves, but that's only a bad thing if you're a servant to the wrong master.

Read Romans 6 v 15–23

ENGAGE YOUR BRAIN

▷ What's the choice of masters on offer? (v16)

▷ What change of ownership has happened to Christians? (v17–18)

Everyone's a slave. When you trust in Jesus, you're set free from one master (sin) to become slave (a willing servant) to another — God. Verse 18 says we've been set free... to become slaves. How does that work???

Read verses 19–23

▷ How should Christians be different from their old sinful selves? (v19)

▷ Did you have more freedom before you became a Christian? (v21)

▷ So what are the benefits of being God's slaves? (v22–23)

Freedom isn't doing as we please: it's doing as God pleases. As our master, sin pays us wages (what we deserve) — death. But God as our master gives us a gift (what we don't deserve) — eternal life. Christians now serve a new boss, so they should live in a way that honours God, and not turn back to their old boss, sin.

THINK IT OVER

Grab another Christian and chew over these questions.

▷ How should being a slave to God affect...
  • what films you watch?
  • how you spend your money?
  • choices you make in life?
  • who you spend time with?

PRAY ABOUT IT

Talk to God about who you're a slave to, and how you're getting along at the mo.

→ TAKE IT FURTHER

Slave away on page 122.

72 | Wedding bells

They make adults cry. They keep dressmakers in business. They make you miss Saturday TV. Paul's talking about weddings.

👁 Read Romans 7 v 1–3

ENGAGE YOUR BRAIN

▷ *What does Paul say about God's Old Testament law? (v1)*

▷ *How does the story (v2–3) back this up?*

A husband and wife promise to be married to each other as long they're both alive. But once of them dies, the marriage is over and they are released from their promise. But Paul's not really talking about weddings — he's making a point about sin and God's law.

👁 Read verses 4–6

▷ *Who do Christians now belong to? (v4)*

▷ *What effect should that have on us? (end of v4)*

▷ *What changes when a person trusts in Jesus? (v5–6)*

A Christian's situation is similar to the widow who remarries. Our old sinful selves have 'died', so we're released from our marriage to the law — trying to meet God's perfect standards. We can't do it. But we don't have to, because Jesus has freed us from sin and death and our old way of life.

Christians are married to Christ. They want to serve Him and bear fruit for God (v4). The law has no hold on them any more. They want to keep God's law and live His way, but they're now free to serve God far more effectively — with the Holy Spirit's help (v6).

PRAY ABOUT IT
Talk to God about how fruitful you are for Him.

THE BOTTOM LINE
Christians are married to Christ.

➡ TAKE IT FURTHER
More fruitiness on page 123.

73 The law on trial

Paul's been talking a lot about God's law. It's been a bit confusing at times. Some people thought Paul was claiming that law-keeping was sinning or caused people to do wrong. Check out his response.

👁 Read Romans 7 v 7–8

ENGAGE YOUR BRAIN

▷ *What does God's law show us? (v7)*

Paul never said that God's law was bad. It came from God, so it can't be wrong. But Paul does say that it isn't enough to save us from sin. If it was, Jesus wouldn't have had to die on the cross.

Ever seen a KEEP OFF THE GRASS sign? Doesn't it make you want to run all over the grass??? Even though you didn't want to before you saw the sign? That's the way sin makes us react to God's law. It tempts us to disobey God's commands.

👁 Read verses 9–13

▷ *How does Paul describe God's law? (v12)*

▷ *So what's the real problem? (v11)*

God's law is *'holy, righteous and good'.* It's perfect — it comes from God. It's our failure to keep God's law that is the problem. God's law shows up our sin. It points out how useless we are at obeying God. That sounds bad, but we need to realise how sinful we are so that we can turn to Jesus to be rescued.

PRAY ABOUT IT

▷ *What sin has God's word shown up in your life?*

Talk to God about it — confessing, repenting and asking for help.

THE BOTTOM LINE

God's law shows up our sin.

→ TAKE IT FURTHER

More law on page 123.

74 Sin inside

Sin can take over people's lives. As much as they want to do what's right, they can't seem to stop themselves from sinning. There's only one answer to the sin problem — Jesus Christ.

👁 Read Romans 7 v 14–17

ENGAGE YOUR BRAIN

▷ *What can rule people's lives? (v17)*

Paul's words can be hard to get your brain around. Here he's saying: *'God's law is perfect and holy. But it couldn't make me holy. Even though I knew God's law, sin was in charge of my life'.*

👁 Read verses 18–25

▷ *What did Paul long for? (v24)*

▷ *What did he need? What's the only way to be free from sin? (v25)*

People's real problem isn't God's law: it's the sin in us. The law can't save us because we can't possibly keep God's law. The sin inside us stops us. Only Jesus and His Spirit living in us can help us please God. Loads more about that in chapter 8.

PRAY ABOUT IT

Talk to God about anything you don't understand from this chapter of Romans. Re-read it, asking God to make it clear and teach you through it. Thank Him that Jesus' death on the cross defeated sin.

→ TAKE IT FURTHER

More about this tricky chapter on page 123.

75 | That's the spirit

As we begin one of the most mind-blowing chapters of the Bible, Paul sums up what he's told us so far. His first sentence is a cracker.

Read Romans 8 v 1–4

ENGAGE YOUR BRAIN

▷ *What must every Christian remember? (v1)*

▷ *What makes this possible? (v2)*

These verses are the flipside to what we were reading yesterday. The gospel (*'the law of the Spirit of life'*) has done what the Old Testament law could never do (v3a) — bring us rescue. And all through Jesus taking God's punishment instead of us (v3b). Christians are not condemned — they won't be punished by God, because Jesus has set them free!

Read verses 5–8

▷ *How does Paul describe people who are ruled by sin?*
v5:
v6:
v7:
v8:

▷ *What about people with God's Spirit in their lives?*
v5:
v6:

If you're a Christian, it should be obvious in the way you live. Your mind is no longer set on doing sinful stuff and it's no longer set against God. Your mind should be set on pleasing God, with the Holy Spirit helping you to live God's way. You're heading for everlasting life and peace with God (v6)!

THINK IT OVER

▷ *Is your life the same as everyone else's?*

▷ *How are you different?*

▷ *How can you please God more?*

PRAY ABOUT IT

Thank God that there is no condemnation for Christians. Talk through the *Think it over* questions with Him.

➡ TAKE IT FURTHER

Check out page 123.

76 | Dead bodies

'Death doesn't really worry me... I just don't want to be there when it happens.' (Woody Allen)
Thoughts about death can fill our minds sometimes. Let's read what Paul said on the subject.

👁 Read Romans 8 v 9–11

ENGAGE YOUR BRAIN

▷ Who's in control of Christians? (v9)

▷ What will happen to their bodies? (v10–11)

All Christians have the Holy Spirit in them, helping them live God's way. Christians' bodies will die, just like everyone else. But God's Spirit raised Jesus from death and He will also give new life to Christians. Their bodies will die but they will go on to live with God for ever.

👁 Read verses 12–17

▷ What does Paul call Christians? (v16)

▷ So how should we live? (v12–13)

▷ What do Christians share in with Jesus? (v17)

Christians are God's children. That means they have to stop being ruled by sin (v12). They're no longer slaves to fear — in fact they can cry out to God their Father ('Abba' means 'Daddy') with their needs (v15). God loves His children.

Christians are also God's heirs, along with His Son, Jesus. The inheritance has an up side and a down side. Christians will share in Christ's sufferings — they will be persecuted for serving God. But they will also share in God's glory — they will one day live with Him and see what He's really like. Phenomenal.

PRAY ABOUT IT

Thank God for the work of His Spirit in us, His children. Tell Him the things you need the Spirit's help to change.

THE BOTTOM LINE

Christians are God's children. Death is not the end for them.

➔ TAKE IT FURTHER

Past, present and future on page 123.

91

77 | Waiting for God

Last time, Paul talked about Christians sharing God's glory. And also sharing Christ's sufferings too. For Christians, the two things go hand in hand. So how do we cope with the tough stuff before eternal glory?

Read Romans 8 v 18–22

ENGAGE YOUR BRAIN

▷ *What does Paul say about our suffering? (v18)*

Life isn't a breeze for Christians. But Christians can always look with certainty to an amazing future. One day God will finish making us more like Him. Christians won't just see God's glory — they'll be part of it!

When sin entered the world through Adam and Eve, God cursed the world (v22). But one day, He will make everything perfect again (v20–21)

Read verses 23–27

▷ *Who else is groaning? (v23)*

▷ *What are Christians waiting for? (v23)*

▷ *Who helps them? How? (v26)*

Believe it or not, Christians aren't happy all the time. We're still waiting for God's rescue plan to be completed. We're waiting to claim our inheritance in eternity with God. We cling on to this certain hope.

As we groan our way through the suffering of this life, we struggle in prayer, barely knowing what to say to God sometimes. The Holy Spirit groans along with us. He understands, and helps us to pray.

PRAY ABOUT IT

Read through today's verses and talk to God about them. Don't know what to say? Then ask God's help.

THE BOTTOM LINE

Current suffering is nothing compared to a future with God.

→ TAKE IT FURTHER

Painful stuff on page 123.

78 | It's all good

— 'Why does God allow such suffering?'
— 'I can't believe God let that happen to a Christian.'
**Ever thought or heard things like that? Well, Paul has
something surprising to say on this topic.**

👁 **Read Romans 8 v 28**

ENGAGE YOUR BRAIN

▷ *What's the surprising truth?*

▷ *How does Paul describe Christians
in this verse?*

Christians are people who love God
— they've been called by Him as
part of His perfect plans. And get
this: God's at work. In all things. For
the good of those who love Him.
Astonishing stuff. This verse puts
things into perspective. Our brief
time of pain on this planet fits into
God's eternal plans. We may not see
it at the time, but God uses the hard
things in life to do us good.

👁 **Read verses 29–30**

▷ *How do this help us understand
how God works everything for
the good of His people?*

God FOREKNEW His people
He knew them intimately and loved
them, even before they were born.

He PREDESTINED them
All Christians have been chosen by
God to be His children forever.

He CALLED them
Christians are called to turn away
from their sinful lives to Jesus.

They're JUSTIFIED too
Put right with God — their sins
cancelled by Jesus' death.

And GLORIFIED
Believers will share in God's glory in
eternity with Him.

God will stop at nothing to make
His people like His perfect Son. and
bring them into glory with Him. Any
suffering will be worth it.

PRAY ABOUT IT
Thank God that however hard life
seems, we can trust Him. His plans
are perfect and will work out.

→ **TAKE IT FURTHER**
More about suffering on page 123.

79 : Winning team

Ever wonder what's the point of being a Christian? Ever worry you might not actually make it to eternal life with God? Can we really be sure? Check out one of the most encouraging Bible passages there is to spur you on.

👁 Read Romans 8 v 31–34

ENGAGE YOUR BRAIN
▷ Why shouldn't Christians worry about opposition? (v31–33)

▷ Where is Jesus now and what is He doing? (v34)

Whoever is against us, God is greater, and He won't abandon us or let us go. He gave up His own Son to rescue us, so of course He will protect us and give everything we could possibly need. No one else can condemn us — God is the ultimate Judge and He has already justified us. Jesus is with God in heaven right now, speaking for us.

Read through those incredible verses again right now, praising God.

👁 Read verses 35–39
▷ What should Christians expect in this life? (v36)

▷ But who can separate them from God? (v35)

▷ What can take eternal life away from them? (v38–39)

Christians will experience suffering and persecution in this life. We must be prepared to face death for Jesus, if necessary (v36). But whatever the opposition, danger or difficulties that tempt us to give up, nothing will separate us from Jesus' love, or from sharing His victory (v37). Jesus isn't just a friend for life, He's a friend for eternal life.

PRAY ABOUT IT
▷ What are you most afraid of?

Add those things to Paul's list in v38–39. And thank God that not even those things can stop His plans or His love for you.

THE BOTTOM LINE
Nothing can separate Christians from God's love.

➡ TAKE IT FURTHER
Cross the winning line on page 124.

80 | Exodus: All washed up

Back to Exodus and God's ground rules for His people, the Israelites. There's a lot here about priests and the tabernacle (huge tent where God was present among His people). But it's relevant to us today too.

👁 Read Exodus 30 v 1–38

ENGAGE YOUR BRAIN

▷ *What amazing privilege are we reminded that the Israelites have? (v6b)*

▷ *What is the danger of that? (see v10, v16, v20)*

▷ *Who do the Israelites belong to? (v12)*

Do you think of yourself as belonging to the Lord? Like the Israelites, if you're a Christian, you are His — twice over. First because He created you and secondly because He redeemed you and paid for your life with the blood of His Son.

▷ *What point are verses 17–21 making?*

The washing was symbolic, as water alone cannot wash away our sin and impurity.

PRAY ABOUT IT

A wise Christian once said: *'We can't be perfect but we can be clean'.*

▷ *Do you make a point of confessing your sin to God every day and asking for His forgiveness?*

▷ *What will you say to Him right now?*

THE BOTTOM LINE

We belong to God.

➡ TAKE IT FURTHER

Wet wet wet — page 124.

81 | Very crafty

What are you good at?
How do you use that ability to serve God?
Do you thank God for the abilities He's given you?

Read Exodus 31 v 1–11

ENGAGE YOUR BRAIN

▷ What does God's Spirit equip Bezalel and Oholiab for?

▷ Does that surprise you?

▷ Why/why not?

▷ Who's in charge? (v6, 11)

Do you ever think that some gifts and abilities are better than others? Check out **1 Corinthians 12 v 28** — helping and administration are just as much gifts of God as other things. Do you thank God for and value the people who print the notice sheet, make food or stack the chairs at your church or youth group?

TALK IT OVER

Read 1 Corinthians 12 v 12–27 with a Christian friend. Ask yourselves honestly whether your behaviour shows that you accept the truth of these verses.

GET ON WITH IT

▷ How can you show appreciation in your prayers and behaviour for the practical gifts God has given Christians you know?

▷ How can you use the abilities God has given you?

THE BOTTOM LINE

God equips His people to serve Him.

TAKE IT FURTHER

Grab the gifts on page 124.

82 Rest day

The Israelites have loads of work to do, preparing the tabernacle. But God still wants His people to take time out on the Sabbath (Saturday, the Jewish holy day).

Read Exodus 31 v 12–18

ENGAGE YOUR BRAIN

▷ *What is the Sabbath to remind the Israelites of? (v13, 17)*

▷ *Why is it so important they remember this?*

TALK IT OVER

We don't have Sabbath days now in the same way as they did back then, but what things can help us to remember those truths about God? Jot down any ideas you have and perhaps discuss it with another Christian.

▷ *Why is the testimony or the law that God gives Moses so special? (v18)*

THINK ABOUT IT

What do you think of 'the law' — all these things you are reading about in Exodus and the following three books of the Bible? Boring? Irrelevant? Confusing? Random?

▷ *If it is given by God, what should our attitude to it be?*

▷ *Do you need to change how you think of it?*

PRAY ABOUT IT

Talk to God about these issues.

THE BOTTOM LINE

God created us and God makes us holy.

➡ TAKE IT FURTHER

Find the truth — on page 124.

83 Holy cow

Moses had been up on that mountain a seriously long time. So what were the rest of the Israelites getting up to in their camp at the bottom of the mountain? Fun and games and campfire songs? Not exactly...

👁 Read Exodus 32 v 1–6

ENGAGE YOUR BRAIN

▶ Why did the Israelites do what they did? (v1)

▶ Does this seem like a good reason to you?

▶ What did it show about their real attitude to God?

▶ Which of the Ten Commandments had they broken?

Do you ever behave anything like the Israelites here? Is it easier to shrink God down to a manageable size, to ignore His right to rule the whole of your life?

TALK IT OVER

Chat with another Christian about ways in which we like to domesticate God — to make Him fit our ideas rather than accepting His ultimate power and authority. Think about your relationships, moral standards and behaviour.

👁 Read verses 7–14

▶ What did Moses plead with God to remember?

There was no point asking God to be merciful on account of the people themselves — they were clearly in the wrong. Moses' only hope was to appeal to God's merciful, forgiving nature.

PRAY ABOUT IT

Is this the basis on which you pray? According to God's character and promises? Are you concerned with His glory and reputation? Spend some time praying about issues in your life from this perspective.

THE BOTTOM LINE

Thank God that He is faithful even when we're not.

➔ TAKE IT FURTHER

Some prayer stuff is on page 124.

84 Facing the consequences

Picture the scene: Moses coming down the mountain with this wonderful, personal, testimony from God in his hands and then seeing idol worship in the Israelite camp. The contrast is terrible and tragic.

👁 Read Exodus 32 v 15–24

ENGAGE YOUR BRAIN

▷ Read verses 15–16 and then read v19. How does the contrast show how horrific the people's sin is?

▷ What do you think of Aaron's excuse? (v22–24)

GET ON WITH IT

Do you make lame excuses when you mess up? From now on, be honest with God and admit it when you've done wrong.

👁 Read verses 25–35

▷ What is Moses' view of the situation? (v25)

▷ How does God deal with their rebellion? (v27–28)

▷ Why can't God ignore this sin?

PRAY ABOUT IT

Moses' plea for his people in v32 is amazing — compare Paul's remark in Romans 9 v 3. Moses was saying: *'Cut me off from yourself, Lord, and spare the people'*. Do you have this depth of feeling for your friends and family who don't believe in Jesus? Pray for them now.

THE BOTTOM LINE

Turning away from the living God is horrific and has horrific consequences.

➔ TAKE IT FURTHER

Idle idols on page 124.

85 | On their own

What will happen next? Will God cut off His rebellious people forever? They deserve it, after all. Will He continue to punish them? How will His promises be fulfilled after this disaster?

👁 Read Exodus 33 v 1–6

ENGAGE YOUR BRAIN

▷ *What does God say to the Israelites? (v1a)*

▷ *Why? (v1b)*

▷ *Why is this amazing after what has just happened?*

▷ *Why is it encouraging for us to know that God keeps His promises?*

▷ *Why is v3 such distressing news to the Israelites?*

All the material blessings in the world are worthless without God. We were made for relationship with Him and without Him there is no lasting peace or happiness.

SHARE IT

A famous Christian statement about the purpose of life goes something like this: *'Man's chief end is to glorify God by enjoying Him forever'*. Think of a way you can talk to a friend this week about what our purpose in life is.

GET ON WITH IT

The Israelites were ruthless about getting rid of anything in their lives that displeased God (see v4–6).
▷ *Do you have the same attitude?*

▷ *Is there something in your life you need to get rid of? Will you start today?*

👁 Read verses 7–11

▷ *Why was this (v11 especially) so amazing?*

THE BOTTOM LINE

We were made to live in relationship with God.

⇥ TAKE IT FURTHER

Scary stuff on page 124.

86 | Glory story

Yet more evidence of God's huge love and mercy in these verses — such a contrast with His faithless people.

👁 Read Exodus 33 v 12–17

ENGAGE YOUR BRAIN

▣ *An amazing place to live but no God, or life in the desert with God — which would Moses prefer? (v15)*

▣ *And you?*

▣ *As Moses prays, what does God promise? (v14–17)*

▣ *How does that answer Moses' fears? (v12, v15-16)*

PRAY ABOUT IT

The end of verse 17 is amazing. If you trust in Christ, then it's true for you too! Thank God now for that.

👁 Read verses 18–23

▣ *What is so striking about God's glory? (v19–23)*

Notice that it's God's goodness and His name that Moses can see and hear but the prospect of seeing God face to face is too much for any human to handle. So what does v11 mean then?

In Jesus we see God's glory (John 1 v 14) and experience His presence with us (Matthew 1 v 22–23). Some Christians think Moses met God's Son (later born as Jesus Christ) in the tent of meeting. It certainly would explain how v11 and v20 can both be true!

PRAY ABOUT IT... AGAIN

Spend time thanking God for the amazing privilege of seeing His glory and having a relationship with Him.

THE BOTTOM LINE

God is glorious and God is with us.

➔ TAKE IT FURTHER

Breathtaking stuff on page 125.

87 New tablets

More grace shown by God today.
Plus a serious warning for His people.
But will they take it to heart?

Read Exodus 34 v 1–9

ENGAGE YOUR BRAIN

▷ How are verses 1–4 a fresh start?

▷ How does God describe Himself in v6–7?

▷ Is this how you think of God?

GET ON WITH IT

Why don't you learn verses 6 and 7 by heart? They are a great reminder of who God is and what He's like.

Read verses 10–28

▷ What great promises does God make in v10–11?

▷ What does He expect His forgiven people to do? (v12-14)

▷ What is the danger in hanging out with the people of that land?

▷ Why must the Israelites be so distinctive?

Verse 16 highlights the dangers of marrying outside the community of believers. It was not that the Canaanites etc were in themselves worse than the Israelites, BUT they would encourage the Israelites to worship other gods and turn away from the one true God who loved them and had rescued them.

Remember the way God describes Himself?

TALK IT OVER

Do you think there are similar dangers for Christians who go out with or marry non-Christians? How might pressure be put on someone's faith in that situation? Talk it through with an older Christian.

THE BOTTOM LINE

God must come first.

→ TAKE IT FURTHER

Historical stuff on page 125.

88 Shiny face

Time for another glimpse of God's holiness. Just look at the effect it had on Moses and the impact it made on God's people.

👁 Read Exodus 34 v 29–35

ENGAGE YOUR BRAIN

▷ Why was Moses' face shining?

▷ How did everyone respond? (v30)

▷ What about Moses — how did he react?

The sheer awesomeness of being in the presence of God rubs off on Moses even, though he isn't aware of it to start with – it's the result of exposure to God's holiness and not related to anything Moses feels personally.

PRAY ABOUT IT

It might not always feel that way, but if you have trusted in Jesus' death and resurrection, then you are holy — you are cleansed, forgiven and God sees you as righteous. Thank Him for that awesome truth now.

GET ON WITH IT

As Christians, we reflect God's glory (see 2 Corinthians 3 v 18). Obviously we aren't going to wander round with towels over our faces, but how can you show something of God's glory to people around you in how you live and speak today?

THE BOTTOM LINE

God is glorious.

➡ TAKE IT FURTHER

Shiny things can be found on page 125.

89 Giving for God

You might remember God saying something about the Sabbath before the golden calf scandal kicked off. We return to the point here which God was making before He was so rudely interrupted...

Read Exodus 35 v 1 – 36 v 7

ENGAGE YOUR BRAIN

▷ *How many times can you spot the phrase 'the LORD commanded'?*

▷ *What does this emphasise about the jobs to be done?*

▷ *How did the Israelites respond?*

▷ *How are their hearts and spirits described?*

It makes a nice change to see the people whole-heartedly wanting to do what God commands.

THINK IT OVER

2 Corinthians 9 v 7 tells us that God loves a cheerful giver.

▷ *Do you cheerfully give your time, your skills, your money?*

▷ *What will you start to give more of to God?*

PRAY ABOUT IT

Talk to God now about your heart and its willingness to serve Him.

THE BOTTOM LINE

Let's obey God willingly.

→ TAKE IT FURTHER

Give it up — page 125.

90 Repeat performance

Having heard all the instructions, the people set about carrying them out. You might want to skim the details here to get an idea of the big picture.

Read Exodus 36 v 8 – 38 v 31

ENGAGE YOUR BRAIN

▷ Why is so much space taken up describing these events when we've already heard about everything in huge detail before?

That's exactly the point! God does not change. He said what He wanted to happen and it does!

▷ Do you notice any difference in the order which the tabernacle and its furnishings are listed this time round?

Last time everything began at the centre — the ark — but this time we see the practical nature of constructing the whole set up and logically you'd start with the tent.

SHARE IT

God always does what He says He will. Look at Mark 8 v 31, 9 v 30–31 and 10 v 32–34. Convinced? Can you talk to someone today about how Jesus' death and resurrection were predicted by Him before they happened?

THE BOTTOM LINE

What God says, happens.

TAKE IT FURTHER

More promises on page 125.

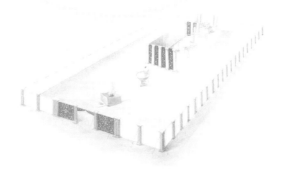

91 | According to plan

Christians can often fall into the trap of thinking that the whole Old Testament is just one big visual aid for our benefit, but let's not forget these were real events and real people.

👁 Skim read Exodus 39 v 1–43

ENGAGE YOUR BRAIN

▷ *What phrase is repeated at the end of each section of this chapter?*

▷ *How had the people carried out God's instructions?*

When Moses first received God's instructions, the Israelites rebelled rather than obeyed. Moses must have thought there was no chance of getting the tabernacle built. So imagine his joy as he toured the workshops and saw everything being made exactly as God commanded.

THINK IT OVER

God's commands for building His church are in the Bible. Imagine God's joy when He sees Christians obeying His commands. Also think about the times we rebel against His commands and do things our own way.

▷ *Which of God's commands are*

you struggling to obey?

👁 Read verses 42–43 again

We've read loads about the tabernacle, and it's been a little repetitive. But it shows just how important the tabernacle was in God's grand scheme. Notice the similarity of v32–43 with Genesis chapter 1, where God created the world and saw that it was good.

God was creating something new here with His tabernacle. It pointed to a new heaven and new earth where He will one day live in perfect harmony with His people for ever. The tabernacle was the beginning of God's way to dwell with His people once again.

PRAY ABOUT IT

Thank God for His plans to live with His people. Ask Him to help you follow His commands.

→ TAKE IT FURTHER

No *Take it Further* section today.

92 | Done and dusted

Well done — you've made it to the end of Exodus!
After all those instructions and despite a major
hold-up, God is ready to dwell in the middle of
His people — see how it happens.

Read Exodus 40 v 1–38

ENGAGE YOUR BRAIN

Take a moment to imagine just
how incredible v34–35 must have
been in reality.

▷ *What has Exodus taught you
about God?*

▷ *And about yourself?*

▷ *Will you follow God single-
mindedly today? And tomorrow?*

As the book of Exodus draws to a
close, we see the Israelites set out on
their travels (v38). What will happen
next? The story is only just beginning.

If you're a Christian, you have taken
part in an even greater Exodus. Think
for a minute and then see if you can
fill in the gaps below.

**The Israelites were slaves to the
Egyptians. Christians were slaves
to _____. (Romans 6 v 6)**

**The Israelites were saved by God's
rescuer, Moses. Christians have
been saved by _____.**

**One day, the Israelites would live
with God in the promised land.
One day, Christians will live with
God in _____.**

PRAY ABOUT IT

Thank God for what He did for Israel.
Thank Him for what He has done, is
doing and will do for those who trust
in Jesus. Thank Him for what you've
learned in the book of Exodus.

THE BOTTOM LINE

God is our Rescuer.

TAKE IT FURTHER

The final *Take it Further* is on
page 125.

TAKE IT FURTHER

EXODUS
The big clean-up

1 – SHORT-TERM MEMORY
Read Romans 6 v 15–23

▷ What did we use to be slaves of? (v17)
▷ Where was that slavery headed? (v16, v21, v23)
▷ Who owns us now?
▷ What are we heading for now? (v22–23)

2 – BIRDS AND BREAD
Amazing though it was, manna was only a warm-up act for the real bread from heaven.

Read John 6 v 25–35

▷ What (or who) is the true bread from heaven?
▷ How is this bread better than manna?

The manna kept the Israelites going day by day for 40 years; the true bread from heaven gives eternal life. Manna was just for Israel — this bread is for the whole world!

3 – ROCK ON!
For some ideas about how to pray honestly when times are tough, read **Psalm 10** or **Psalm 13** (there are many others!) and use them as the basis of your own prayers.

Read Exodus 17 v 6 and then 1 Corinthians 10 v 3–4

Because God stands before the rock, it means that Moses strikes through God when he strikes the rock. Then God's grace is poured out. This somehow points us to the cross. When Paul, in 1 Corinthians, says the rock is Christ, we are reminded that Christ being 'struck' on the cross so that we can receive God's grace.

4 – HANDS UP!
The words of the Anglican baptism service include the line: *'Fight bravely under the banner of Christ against the world, the flesh and the devil and continue his faithful soldier and servant to the end of your life'*. Pray for God's help today in doing exactly that.

5 – IN-LAWS AND OUTLAWS

Make a list of all that God has done for you through Christ (**Ephesians 1 v 3–14** is a good place to help you get started). Add all the material things He has blessed you with in your life now. Then add any specific answers to prayer etc.

Keep it somewhere you can look at it when you need to remember how good God has been to you.

6 – GET READY

Read Hebrews 12 v 18–29

Wonder at it and pray in response to it.

7 – STARTER FOR TEN

▶ *Failing to obey the first commandment is a good definition of 'sin'. Do you agree?*

Read Romans 1 v 18–23

▶ *Can you see that tendency in your own life and in the world around you?*
▶ *What will you do about it?*

8 – REMEMBER GOD

▶ *What are the pros and cons of having a day of rest every week?*

Maybe you could chat it through with a Christian friend. Things you might like to discuss are:

– having a rest/break each week
– not working on a Sunday (if you're employed)
– being able to have a central meeting with other Christians
– not shopping and being materialistic.

Alternatively, what are the dangers of treating only one day as 'holy' or becoming legalistic/restricted by rules that aren't in the New Testament?

9 – THE FINAL SIX

Read Mark 12 v 30

▶ *Do you do that?*
▶ *Really?*

Spend some time working through each of those areas and thinking through what loving God with that part of you would look like in practice. Then pray for His forgiveness and help to do it.

10 – POWERFUL GOD

Spend some time dwelling on God's holiness.

Read Isaiah 6 v 1–7

▶ *What did Isaiah see? (v1)*
▶ *What does this tell us about God?*
▶ *What shows the heavenly beings' (seraphs) reverence for God? (v2)*
▶ *What did they acknowledge about God? (v3)*
▶ *What was the effect of God's presence?*

Read Job 40 v 1 – 42 v 6 for a further reminder of God's greatness, power and holiness.

11 – SERVING SERVANTS

For more on the topic of slavery see Galatians 3 v 26–29.

Then read Ephesians 6 v 5–9
> *What principles here might apply to work or school?*
> *How obedient should we be? (v5)*
> *When should we work hard? (v6)*
> *Why? (v6–8)*
> *What's the deal for bosses? (v9)*

12 – REVENGE ISN'T SWEET

Check out Matthew 5 v 11–12 and v 38–42
> *What do you find most difficult about not retaliating when people treat you badly?*
> *How can Jesus' example help you?*
> *How will you respond when people mistreat you because you're a Christian?*

Now read 1 Peter 3 v 13–16

ROMANS
Basic Christianity

13 – DEAR ROMANS...
Read verse 2
> *Would you say that the Old Testament is important?*
> *Why should we, according to v2?*

Read verse 5
> *Can we accept Jesus' rescue but not*

change how we live?
> *Can we accept Him as Saviour but not as Lord of our lives?*
> *Why not? How do v4–5 help on this?*
> *Are you trusting Jesus and obeying Him?*

14 – THE POWER OF GOD
Read verse 11 again
It's not obvious what *'the gift'* is — but Paul's aim would be to see their needs and build them up as Christians.
> *How serious was Paul about his gospel work? (v9)*
> *What's worth imitating about his prayer? (v10)*

Read verse 16
Grab some paper and make a list of your non-Christian friends and family. Do you ever think some of them aren't 'at the right stage' for you to talk about the gospel with them? Or maybe don't even need it?
> *What would Paul say?*
> *So, how will you make progress with those friends?*

Jesus knew that His followers would sometimes be ashamed of Him — but He said we had every reason not to be.
Read Mark 8 v 38 and 2 Timothy 1 v 8–12

How are you feeling now? Talk to God about what's on your mind and ask Him to help you stick by the gospel.

15 – NO EXCUSES
Read verse 20 again
God's creation reveals HIm and His power to everyone.

Read how Psalm 19 v 1–6 puts it and then read John 1 v 1, 14, 18
▷ *How does Jesus reveal God to us far more fully?*

16 – TRAMPLING TRUTH
Read verses 26–27
So what's Paul saying about homosexual behaviour?

1. It displeases God. It's a result of God's wrath ('God gave them over to...') so it must displease God.

2. It's against His created order. 'Unnatural' here means 'against the way God created us'.

Check out: Genesis 1 v 27–28
    Genesis 2 v 24
    Matthew 19 v 4–6
    Leviticus 18 v 22

17 – PASSING JUDGMENT
Read verse 1 again
The old line that 'when you point a finger at someone else, you've got three pointing back at you' is completely true.

▷ *How do you fall into the trap of setting incredibly high standards for others but low ones for yourself?*
▷ *When you last criticised someone else,*

how much of that criticism could have been directed at you?

Read verse 5
The day of God's wrath is not to be treated lightly. It's terrifying.
▷ *How should it affect your behaviour today/tomorrow/next week?*

18 – JUSTICE FOR ALL
Read verse 16 again
When Paul mentions *'secrets'* he's not talking about surprise birthday party plans, He means wrong motives, fantasies, thoughts we hide.

▷ *What secrets will you confess to God right now and then leave behind?*

Read John 5 v 22–30

19 – PRACTISE WHAT YOU PREACH
For more on circumcision and obedience to God...

Read Genesis 17 v 9–14, then Deuteronomy 30 v 6, and finally Colossians 2 v 9–12

20 – WHAT'S THE POINT?
Read Job 40 v 1–14
▷ *Is anyone as powerful as God? (v9)*
▷ *Could Job dish out justice like God? (v10–12)*
▷ *Can anyone save themselves? (v14)*

Read Psalm 111
▷ *How would you describe God from*

the words of this psalm?
▶ *Is God faithful to His promises? (v7–8)*
▶ *Is He fair and just? (v7)*

21 – NO ONE'S PERFECT

Think what excuses we make to pretend we're OK with God.
'I'm not as bad as a criminal.'
'I can't help my human nature – I was born this way.'
'I can't really be expected to keep God's perfect standards.'
'I do some pretty good things which God must like.'

▶ *Do you hide behind any of these?*
▶ *Can you think of any others?*
▶ *How does Romans 1–3 shoot down all these excuses?*

All around us there are people who know enough about God that they have no excuse for rejecting Him.
▶ *Where does v19's verdict leave your non-Christian friends?*
▶ *What should it make Christians do?*

22 – GOD'S FREE GIFT
Read verses 21–22
Most other religions say we can save ourselves. *'Do this... and you'll be OK with God.'*
▶ *Now see why the gospel is great news?*

This is amazing stuff. The cross wasn't emergency plan B, as if God was caught by surprise by our rejection of Him. No, it was always part of His plan, announced in advance in the Old Testament.
▶ *How great does this make God?*

23 – FAITH THE FACTS

Read Jesus' conversation with a Jewish guy who thought he was OK with God
— John 3 v 1–21

▶ *How did Jesus shake up Nic's thinking? (v3–4)*
▶ *What did he need to realise? (v5–8)*
▶ *Why should Nic' have known these things? (v10)*
▶ *How does Jesus use the Old Testament to convince this Jewish leader? (v11–15)*
▶ *What is Jesus' big message? (v15–18)*
▶ *What's the big choice? (v19–21)*

24 – FAITH WORKS
Read Genesis 15 v 1–6
▶ *As Abraham's shield, how was God saying He would help him?*
▶ *God is also his great reward. How would this reassure Abraham?*

Abraham believed and trusted God, and God accepted him. It's one of the great moments in the Old Testament. It's true for us too. As we trust God to forgive us through what Jesus has done, He counts us as being right with Him.
▶ *How do you show that you trust God?*

25 – SHOWING PROMISE

Let's see what Jesus said about all this.
Read John 8 v 31–41

▷ *What's the mark of a real disciple? (v31)*
▷ *What's the promise for them? (v32)*
▷ *What hadn't these Jews understood? (v33–36)*

26 – CREDIT NOTE

Summary of Romans 1–4

Paul, using evidence from the Old Testament, has said that everyone has sinned, whether Jew or Gentile. Everyone has failed to meet God's perfect standards.

The only way to become right with God is through faith (just like Abraham) in God's promised Saviour.

▷ *If someone asked how you know you are saved, how would you answer?*
▷ *Read Romans 4 v 24–25. Does your answer show your faith is resting on the right thing?*

27 – PEACE AND JOY

Read Colossians 1 v –22

▷ *Despite being God's Son, what was Jesus prepared to do? (v20)*
▷ *What are people like before they become Christians? (v21)*
▷ *And after? (v22)*

28 – NO PAIN NO GAIN

Read 1 Peter 4 v 12–19

▷ *Should Christians be surprised to be suffering? (v12)*
▷ *Why should Christians praise God for their suffering? (v13)*
▷ *Why else? (v14)*
▷ *Why else? (v16–18)*
▷ *What's Peter's final command? (v19)*

29 – UNBEATABLE LOVE

Read verses 5–11 again

▷ *Why should Christians be the most positive people around?*
▷ *How do you shape up in that respect?*
▷ *And what if life gets tougher?*

Now read some more stunning truths from Paul in **Romans 8 v 28–39**

LUKE
Jesus: the early years

30 – DUMBSTRUCK

Luke doesn't just write a record of the events, but an explanation of them too. Describing them as *'the things that have been fulfilled'* shows what he thinks of them.

Some people say: 'This makes bad history because history should simply be a record of events.' But all history is events plus explanation. Just by choosing which events to record, the writer is explaining what he thinks is important. What makes it a good history is if the writer's explanation is correct.

Read verse 17 and then Malachi 4 v 5–6 and 3 v 1
Malachi spoke of a figure like Elijah and of a messenger who would prepare the way for the Lord. By drawing the reader's attention to these Old Testament prophecies in v17, Luke is dropping clues as to what would happen next.

God working in history is a big thing for Luke. Almost every incident in chapters 1–4 contains a reference to the Old Testament. Luke's saying that God was fulfilling what He had promised.

31 – PREGNANT PAUSE
Read verses 31–33 again
The name Jesus means 'God saves' — which is the big theme of the Gospel of Luke. Jesus is the Saviour of the world.

Jesus is the greatest ruler the world has ever seen (v33). People enter Jesus' kingdom when they let Him rule their lives as King.
▶ *What areas of your life do you try to hold back from Jesus' rule?*

32 – BUMP JUMP
Read verse 47
Mary was in a position of special honour, but it's important not to overdo this honour. Don't build her up into a godlike figure. There is no suggestion that she herself was without sin: she knew that

she too needed a Saviour.

In her song, Mary looked back to what God had done and forward to what He would do.
▶ *When life's hard, how does it change your view if you look back (to the cross) and forward (to eternal life)?*

For example, sometimes we can feel we've got lots of problems and doubt whether God cares about us. Jesus' death on the cross tells us that He does — hugely. The prospect of living with God eternally reminds us to keep going with God when it's hard.
▶ *Think how looking back and forward like this helps when you're feeling happy, sad, guilty, unsure, afraid, angry or impatient.*

33 – FAMILY FORTUNES
Read verses 71–73
God acted to keep His past promises. In particular, the promises He originally gave to Abraham (v73) which dominate the Old Testament and were still waiting to be fulfilled in the New Testament.

Read Genesis 12 v 1–3
God promised Abraham a land (Canaan), a people (the Israelites), a blessing (the presence of God) and through him, a blessing to the nations. Zechariah was still waiting to see God's people living in God's place under God's blessing and being a blessing to other nations. We'll soon see that Jesus is God's blessing to the world.

34 – ANGEL DELIGHT

Do you want to speak about Jesus, but find it hard? Here's some help: ask God to make you excited about what Jesus has done and about living for Him.

Spend time working out what to say (use v11–12, v14). Try it out on a Christian friend. Imagine being asked: *'Christmas? It's more about Santa than Jesus, isn't it?'*

Pray for a chance to talk to your non–Christian friends.

35 –SIMEON AND ANNA

What's all this about consolation and redemption? It's all to do with the exile: the people of Israel and Judah were removed from their land for failing to obey God. In His mercy, God promised them comfort and a return home. And it happened.

But Simeon and Anna knew knew the exile hadn't really ended yet. Even though some of the people were back in the land of Israel, they were still far from God. Some Israelites were still looking for God to bring His people home, back to Himself. Simeon and Anna saw God would do that through Jesus.

Read verses 34–35

▶ *What will you say to friends who believe Jesus was basically just a nice, harmless, religious man?*

▶ *Why was there such strong opposition to Him?*

36 – MISSING JESUS

Read verse 49 again

These are Jesus' first recorded words. They're a statement about His relationship with God. It's different and deeper than anything that had been known before. Luke will later tell us it's a relationship into which Jesus will bring all others who put their faith in Him. Because of Jesus, Christians have a close relationship with God and can talk with Him.

Luke 11 v 1–4

▶ *How should you speak to God?*

▶ *What attitude should you have?*

▶ *What things should you pray for?*

▶ *What else do you need to ask God about?*

Now do it.

37 – DESERT STORM

Verses 1–2 tell us that this happened around 28–29AD. A *tetrarch* was a ruler.

Read verse 4

Luke quotes Isaiah 40 v 3–5. Remember Simeon and Anna (from chapter 2), waiting for comfort? Isaiah 40 begins: *'Comfort, comfort my people, says your God.'* (Read it some time.) John confirms what they'd discovered — God is acting to bring His people back to Himself.

Baptism (before Jesus came) was the way Gentiles would become Jews. But when John said Jews needed it too (v3), he was saying that no one could claim they were OK with God because of their background. Ouch! **Everyone** had to repent.

Read verse 16
and then Ephesians 1 v 13–14
God gave the Holy Spirit at Pentecost (read about it in Acts 2). The Spirit now lives in every Christian, ensuring rescue from God's judgment.

Read Luke 3 v 19–20
John's preaching made people hostile towards Him.
How does this warn and encourage us when we talk to others about Jesus?

Read Psalm 2 v 6–7
then Exodus 4 v 22–23
and Isaiah 42 v 1
and then Isaiah 52 v 13 – 53 v 12
What do these verses tell us about Jesus?

Read Luke 1 v 38
Jesus' family tree (or genealogy) goes right back not just to David, or Abraham, but Adam. Jesus is being identified not just with Jews, but all people.

Read verse 13 again
Jesus may well have faced more temptations from Satan than these three, but these are the only ones Luke records. Notice that Jesus was in the desert. It was in the desert that the Israelites gave in to

temptation, grumbled and turned their back on God (Numbers 14 v 1–38). Here in the desert, Jesus does the opposite.

Remember Genesis too? The tempter challenged Adam and Eve to doubt God's word and they gave in (The Fall — Genesis 3 v 1–13). Here, Jesus was being tempted in the same way but not giving in. He's man as man should be, totally obedient to God.

It's the first time in history that a son of Adam has confronted the devil's temptations and won. Jesus succeeded where Adam failed — He's the true Son of God. He would go on to defeat the devil ultimately by His death and resurrection. Jesus reversed the effects of human sin and the Fall. By the cross, Jesus re-opened the way to God and saved us from God's punishment. Incredible.

You can read about Elijah and Elisha in 1 Kings 17 and 2 Kings 5.

Read Luke 4 v 22
"Isn't this Joseph's son?" The answer has to be 'Yes, but far more than just Joseph's son.' Luke wants us to learn from his opening chapters that Jesus is the Son of God, and His salvation is not just for Nazareth or Israel, but for the world.

He warns His home town, saying: 'Look, your own history warns you of the possibility of being rejected while others (non-Jews) are blessed.' No wonder they were angry!

▷ *How does it help knowing that friends you talk to about Jesus may react strongly when you do?*

Don't be put off if they do — it's to be expected, isn't it? Keep praying for them.

42 – SPIRIT SPLATTER
Read verse 35

Jesus told the evil spirit to be quiet because He wanted people to understand why He came. Otherwise they might follow Him for the wrong reasons: because they loved to see miracles or thought He'd beat the Romans. People had to grasp not just who Jesus was but what His job was, too. He came to save them from sin.

43 – SICKNESS AND DEMONS

Catch up on what Luke's already told us about the good news and the kingdom of God:

Luke 1 v 32, 68–70, 74–77
Luke 2 v 10–11, 29–32
Luke 3 v 16–17
Luke 4 v 18–19
▷ *Why is it good news?*
▷ *Who is the King?*

44 – IT'S SIMPLE, SIMON

Sometimes it's said of Christians: *'Oh they go to church on Sundays, but they're no different to anyone else the rest of the week.'* Simon was happy to

let Jesus preach from his boat, but then suddenly Jesus told him how to fish. But Simon listened and let Jesus change his life forever.

We've got to do the same. We must follow Jesus and let Him rule all the time: in our work (school, college or job), in our time off, in our sport, in our relationships, in our going out, in our internet use, in the way we spend money....

Read Luke 9 v 23–26
▷ *How should Jesus rule over different parts of your life?*

45 – SKIN DEEP
Read verse 16

Crowds were flocking to Jesus, but He *'withdrew to lonely places and prayed'*.
▷ *Why did He do that?*
▷ *How can you copy Jesus' example?*

Make a list of things that distract you from praying. Now resolve to stop them getting in the way of prayer. And be realistic — most of us resolve to pray regularly, then find we've given up after a day or so. How will you be different?

46 – DROPPING IN
Read verse 17

The word *Pharisee* literally means *'the separated ones'*. They saw themselves as a special, separate group, trying to keep God's laws. The aim was good, but they went wrong in two ways. They created a huge system of detailed rules which they said people had to obey (like a list of 39 things you couldn't do on the Sabbath). And they looked down on everyone else for not being so religious. Jesus' words were upsetting them already. More of that to come!

Read verse 24
Jesus described himself for the first time as the *Son of Man* — a title taken from the book of Daniel (chapter 7 v 13–14). It referred to the coming Messiah. So Jesus is saying: *'That's who I am!'*

48 – FAST AND FURIOUS
Read Isaiah 58 v 3–11
▶ *What was the problem with the way these people (the Israelites) fasted? (v3–4)*
▶ *What else should they have been doing? (v6–7)*
▶ *What would be the result if they obeyed God rather than doing things to look good? (v8–11)*
▶ *Is there anything you do to look good, to look more holy?*
▶ *Is there anything you don't do that you should be doing?*

EXODUS

49 – PAYBACK TIME
Although we should respect other people's property and possessions, Christians' attitude to their stuff should be radically different to everyone else's.

Read Matthew 6 v 19-34
▶ *How does this challenge you?*

50 – LOADS OF LAWS
Because God is holy, He wants His people to be holy.
▶ *Can you see any contrasts in these verses between the way the nations around them (including Egypt) would have behaved and the way God wanted the Israelites to live?*

51 – FESTIVAL SEASON
Read verse 15
'No one is to appear before me empty-handed.'
▶ *How does that principle apply to believers today?*

Read Romans 12 v 1–2 and Philippians 4 v 18
▶ *What kind of offerings is God looking for from you?*
▶ *As you meet with God's people (other Christians), do you have a getting mind-set or a serving mind-set?*

52 – GUARDIAN ANGEL
See how Romans 8 v 1-17 changes everything.

It's complicated reading but work out:
a) our status as Christians before God
b) how we can meet God's standards
c) our heart's desire
d) how God's Spirit helps us to live for Him

53 – HOLY SMOKE

**Look at verses 3 and 7 again
and then read Matthew 21 v 28–32**

▶ *What does God really want from
His people?*

▶ *Which of the two sons do you tend to
be more like?*

▶ *Anything you need to pray about?*

54 – LIVE-IN LORD

Have a look at John 1v14 — 'made
his dwelling among us' is literally
'tabernacled among us' — set up
His tent.

Read all of John 1 v 1–18

▶ *List some of the reasons why this was
such an amazing event.*

v3:

v4:

v9:

v13:

v14:

v16:

v17:

v18:

55 – THE MERCY SEAT

Read Romans 7 v 7-25
Sometimes God's law in the Old Testament
gets a bad press, as if it was all negative
and full of rules.

▶ *But what does Paul say about God's
law:*

- *Its character? (v12)*
- *Its purpose? (v7 and v13)*
- *Its limitations? (v22-24)*
- *How we can satisfy its requirements?
(Romans 8 v 1-4)*

56 – TABLE MANNERS

The bread of the presence crops up a
couple of times after this.

**Read 1 Samuel 21 v 1–6
and then Luke 6 v 1–5**

▶ *What do we learn about the rules
about this bread?*

▶ *What does Jesus' remark add?*

57 – SEE THE LIGHT

Read verses 31–33
The lamp is designed to look like an
almond tree, the first tree that blossomed
each year.

Read verse 37
In Old Testament times, 7 was a
number that symbolised perfection and
completeness. It crops up loads in Exodus
and especially in Revelation.

Read Psalm 27 v 1

▶ *How is the Lord a light for you?*

▶ *What can you do to live more in
the light?*

Read Hebrews 9 v 1–10
- *Who alone could enter God's presence? (v6–7)*
- *How often?*
- *Why did he have to bring blood?*

Read Hebrews 9 v 11–15
- *What sacrifice did Jesus offer? (v12)*
- *What did it achieve? (v12, v14–15)*
- *Does it have to happen every year or will it last forever? (v12)*
- *What should it encourage us to do? (end of v14)*

59 – AT THE ALTAR
- *Do you take sin seriously enough?*
- *Do your non-Christian friends or family?*
- *Can you explain that Jesus had to die because that is what we deserve for our rebellion against God?*
- *Try working on how you can get across such vital truth.*

60 – PRIESTS ON THE CATWALK
Time to fill the gaps.

Read Exodus 28 v 15–30
This time Israel's names were engraved 'on the heart'. The high priest not only had the weight of responsibility on his shoulders, but the love of the people on his heart. And the mysterious Urim and Thummim would be the means of guiding the people in God's ways — as well as bringing the people to God, the priests would have the job of bringing God to the people.

Read Exodus 29 v 1–9 and then 1 Peter 2 v 5 and 9
All true believers are ordained ministers! They are washed in Jesus' blood, clothed in His righteousness and anointed by the Holy Spirit to equip them to serve Him in the world. Together we are God's priests, 'ordained' to bring God to the world and the world to God.

PSALMS 25–30

61 – SHAMELESS
Check out 1 Peter 5 v 8–11
- *What do these verses teach us about our enemy the devil?*
- *What should we do as we fight against the devil? (v8–9)*
- *Why?*
- *What will God do as we fight the devil? (v10)*

Praise God He has the power to make us strong, firm and steadfast against the devil. Does that mean we sit back and do nothing? No! We've still got to work hard at resisting him through prayer, reading and following the Bible, hanging out with other Christians, and not putting ourselves in situations where we know Satan is going to try and trip us up. It's over to you…

62 – CLEAR-CUT CHRISTIAN
Read Colossians 3 v 1-11
▷ *What does it say we should put to death?*

▷ *Why?*

▷ *What must we get rid of?*

▷ *Why?*

▷ *Are your heart and mind set on things above or dragged down to earth by sinful practices?*

63 – CROSS-EYED
Read 1 Peter 1 v 3-5
▷ *What has God's great mercy given us?*

▷ *Through what?*

▷ *Into what?*

▷ *How can Christians be sure they'll get eternal life? (v5)*

Use these verses to talk to God, praising Him for all He has mercifully given us through Jesus.

64 – THE SHIELD
Read John 3 v 16–18
God's greatest work was sending Jesus to the world.

▷ *Why did God send Jesus? (v16)*

▷ *How does Jesus hold the key to eternal life? (v16)*

▷ *Why was Jesus sent? (v17)*

▷ *What is the difference between those who believe in Jesus and those who don't? (v18)*

65 – STORMIN' STUFF
We can see the power and majesty of God in a thunder storm, and learn something of His splendour just as David did. The primary place God speaks to us, however, is in His word.

Read Psalm 119 v 89–112
(You may particularly like v99 – yes, if you are trusting in God and your teachers aren't, you have more insight than all of them, because God's word is the true source of wisdom!)

▷ *Do these verses echo your own beliefs about God's word and your own determination to follow it?*

Praise God that He has communicated so clearly and lovingly to us through His word, the Bible.

66 – ROLLERCOASTER PSALM
In this psalm, David seems to have been healed of some great illness.

Read Luke 17 v 11-19
▷ *Here are ten lepers whom Jesus heals of leprosy. How do they respond differently to the healing?*

The guy who comes back to thank Jesus was a Samaritan. Jesus was a Jew and Samaritans were arch-enemies of Jews. We were once God's enemies because of our sin (see Romans 5 v 10) and yet God has healed us of our 'sin disease'.

▷ *Are you thankful, like the Samaritan,*

for all God has done for you?
▶ *How do you show it?*

If you want to look into the whole mind-blowing sainthood thing some more, check out:
Romans 8 v 27,
Psalm 34 v 9
and Psalm 116 v 15

ROMANS

67 – SIN DISEASE
Read verse 12 again
Verse 12 is left unfinished, but verse 18 kinda finishes it off.

Read verses 13–14
Because of sin, death was let loose on everyone. Verse 13 doesn't mean that sin didn't matter before the law was given by God to Moses. The law actually showed sin up so that we could recognise it for what it is, and recognise ourselves for what we are — sinners in need of Jesus.

68 – FULL OF LIFE
Read Galatians 3 v 19–25
▶ *What does God's perfect law alert us to? (v22)*
▶ *What should it lead us to do? (v22, 24)*
▶ *Why?*

69 – EVIL TWIN
Read verses 3–4
The New Testament assumed believers would be baptised when they started to trust Jesus. The two events were almost considered part of one event. Baptism was not a way to become a follower of Christ, but it showed your faith in Him.

Christians still get baptised today. Baptism is a graphic picture of the death and resurrection that happens when you trust Jesus — going down in the water symbolises the death of your sinful life; coming back up symbolises being raised to eternal life with Jesus. It's also a public statement of your faith, for all to see.

70 – ALIVE AND KICKING
Want even more practical advice on battling against sin? Then check out these Bible passages and pray about the issues they raise...
Matthew 12 v 34–37
Ephesians 5 v 3–4
Matthew 15 v 19–20
1 John 2 v 15–17

71 – SLAVING AWAY
Read verse 16
Trusting Jesus (becoming a Christian) is an act of self-surrender (v16). So, of course, it leads to slavery to God. Slavery demands radical, total obedience.
▶ *What challenge does Matthew 6 v 24 throw at you?*

Now try learning Romans 6 v 23 by heart.

72 – WEDDING BELLS
Read Galatians 5 v 22–23
▶ *Which of those fruit are in your life?*
▶ *Which do you need to work on?*

73 – THE LAW ON TRIAL
Read Exodus 20 v 1–21
▶ *Which of the Ten Commandments really hit you hard?*
▶ *What do you need to do about it?*
▶ *What do you need to say to God?*

74 – SIN INSIDE
There's been a big debate about Romans chapter 7. The question is: Who is the 'wretched man' in v24 and the 'I' of v14–25. A lot of people think it's either:
a) a Jew who's not become a Christian
b) a Jew who's in the process of becoming a Christian, or
c) a Christian.

I tend to lean towards option b). It isn't someone completely separated from God, but he also doesn't seem to be free from slavery to sin. It seems to be Paul looking back to before he was saved by Jesus. (See Romans 6 v 15–23.)

Read through chapters 6 and 7 again and work out what *you* think.

75 – THAT'S THE SPIRIT
Read verses 3–4
The law couldn't justify us or make us holy or right with God. It couldn't change our sinful nature. But God took the initiative — it's all down to Him!

Try explaining v3–4 in your own words. How would you get the message across to a non-Christian mate or family member?

76 – DEAD BODIES
Read verses 12–13 again and then Colossians 3 v 1–10
▶ *What's a Christian's past, present and future? (v3–4)*
▶ *So how should that affect them? (v1–2)*
▶ *What practical things from v5–10 do you need to deal with?*

77 – WAITING FOR GOD
Read verse 22
'Pains of childbirth' — these are not just intense pains (ask your mum), they also show that something new is coming.

It's been said that *'Some Christians grin too much and groan too little.'*
▶ *Do you think that's true?*

Read verses 26–27
It's not saying we grunt or groan when we're praying. It's saying that God's Spirit prays for us. And He longs for the day when we'll be free from our current sufferings. Great stuff.

78 – IT'S ALL GOOD
Read 1 Peter 1 v 1–7
▶ *How does Peter describe Christians? (v1)*
▶ *Who chose them? (v2)*
▶ *How does Peter describe a Christian's life? (v2)*

▶ What can Christians look forward to? (v3–5)

▶ How can Christians be sure of eternal life? (v5)

▶ What will happen in the meantime? (v6)

▶ Why must we suffer? (v7)

Now talk to God.

79 – WINNING TEAM

Well done for reaching the end of Romans 1–8. We'll tackle chapters 9–16 in issue 5.

▶ What has God taught you from Romans 1–8?

EXODUS   80 – ALL WASHED UP

The water used by the priests was just a picture of the ultimate truth we read about in **Hebrews 10 v 19–22**.

▶ What blessings do Christians have?

▶ What should our response be? (v22)

81 – VERY CRAFTY

Look at 1 Corinthians 12 v 1–11

▶ Who are the gifts from?

▶ Who is gifted?

▶ Are God's gifts only for more 'spiritual' Christians?

▶ Why are the gifts given?

▶ Any room for selfish pride or jealousy?

82 – REST DAY

Read 2 Timothy 3 v 16–17

▶ What do we learn about the whole of the Bible?

▶ Have you accepted that truth?

▶ What has Exodus been teaching you?

83 – HOLY COW

There are lots of examples in the Bible of people praying on the strength of who God is and His promises rather than on their own merits.

Check out Genesis 18 v 20–26 and 2 Kings 19 v 14–18

▶ What can you learn from this way of praying?

84 – FACING THE CONSEQUENCES

You might not think you worship idols — no statues or golden calves in your house! Or perhaps your family comes from a culture where people do worship idols. But idolatry can be more subtle than that too.

Read Colossians 3 v 5

▶ Do you think of these things as idolatry?

▶ How do they replace God as something we worship?

▶ What do you put before God in your life?

▶ What will you do about it?

85 – ON THEIR OWN

Read Luke 16 v 19–31

The worst thing about hell is that people will be cut off from God completely (see v26).

Pray for people you know who are not currently trusting in Jesus. Ask God to open their eyes to the truth and give you opportunities to share the good news of Jesus' death and resurrection with them.

86 – GLORY STORY

Look at verse 19 again

It's a pretty profound statement about God. Paul quotes it in Romans 9 v 15. Think about it and ask yourself these questions:

▶ *Does anyone deserve God's mercy?*
▶ *Why does God choose some people and seemingly not others?*

Discuss this issue with an older Christian if you need to.

87 – NEW TABLETS

Read 1 Kings 11 v 1–13

▶ *What did Solomon do wrong? (v1–2)*
▶ *Who influenced who? (v4)*
▶ *In what way? (v5)*
▶ *What was God's verdict on him? (v6)*
▶ *How far did Solomon go in his idolatry? (v7–8)*
▶ *Why did God have every right to be angry? (v9–10)*
▶ *What would God do? (v11)*
▶ *And not do? (v12–13)*
▶ *What can you learn from Solomon's experience?*
▶ *What do you need to change in your life?*

88 – SHINY FACE

Read 2 Corinthians 3 v 7–18

▶ *What is the difference between the glory on Moses' face and the glory we have experienced as Christians? (v7–8,*
v10–11)
▶ *What is the amazing truth about you (v18) if you have God's Spirit (all Christians do!)?*

89 – GIVING FOR GOD

▶ **Read 2 Corinthians 8 v 1–9**

▶ *How are the Macedonian churches described?*
▶ *Why might their behaviour and attitude be unexpected?*
▶ *Does this challenge your attitude towards giving?*
▶ *What is the basis for all of our giving? (v9)*

90 – REPEAT PERFORMANCE

If what God says always happens, it gives us great confidence in His promises.

▶ *Which of God's promises do you have confidence in?*

Try Philippians 1 v 6 and 1 Corinthians 10 v 13 for starters.

92 – DONE AND DUSTED

After ending on a high note, it's not long before things start going downhill. In fact ,once Israel had fallen as low as they could, it became clear that a new Exodus would be needed.

Read Jeremiah 31 v 31–34

It's just one of many passages from the Old Testament prophetic books which looks forward to Jesus and the new Exodus.

engage wants to hear from YOU!

▷ Share experiences of God at work in your life
▷ Any questions you have about the Bible or the Christian life?
▷ How can we make *engage* even better?

Email us — **engage@thegoodbook.com**

Or use the space below to write us a quick note. You can post it to:

engage 37 Elm Road, New Malden, Surrey, KT3 3HB, UK

In the next engage

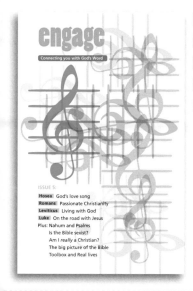

Hosea God's love song
Romans Passionate Christianity
Leviticus Living with God
Luke On the road with Jesus
Plus: Nahum and Psalms
   Is the Bible sexist?
   Am I *really* a Christian?
   The big picture of the Bible
   Toolbox and Real lives

Order engage now!

Make sure you order the next issue of engage. Or even better, grab a one-year subscription to make sure engage plops through your letterbox as soon as it's out.

Call us to order in the UK on 0845 225 0880
International: +44 (0) 20 8942 0880

or visit your friendly neighbourhood website:
UK: www.thegoodbook.co.uk
N America: www.thegoodbook.com
Australia: www.thegoodbook.com.au

CY

CY is the evangelistic course for **young people** in the **21st century.**

'CY is a brilliant course for teenagers who are wanting to find out about the claims of Christ. It is Biblically based and presented in a clear and fun way that is understandable to teenagers without detracting from the wonderful truths it presents'. EMILY JOHNSTON, YOUTHWORKER

Seven dynamic and innovative sessions present the gospel clearly to your youth group and their friends.

Take your young people on a journey through Mark's Gospel. They'll **CY** Jesus Matters, **CY** Jesus Died, **CY** Jesus Lives – and much more.

With specially written talks, Bible studies, discussion starters, activities and the optional use of the Christianity Explored DVDs, **CY** helps young people to make the ultimate discovery.

Visit www.christianityexplored.com/cy

UK: www.thegoodbook.co.uk
N America: www.thegoodbook.com
Australia: www.thegoodbook.com.au